RETIREMENT MADE S.I.M.P.L.E. :

Six Steps to a Successful Retirement!

By

Terry D. Higdon

RETIREMENT MADE S.I.M.P.L.E. :

Six Steps to a Successful Retirement!

Printed in the United States of America
Year of First Printing: 2020

ACKNOWLEDGMENTS

To my existing clients, and their families for allowing me to help them reach their financial goals. You have inspired me to always be the best person I can be! Thank you!

To all those who have coached me whether in sports or in life. Thank you for your thoughtful education and for helping me to realize that life isn't about me but about everyone with whom I come into contact!

To my cousin James Franklin "Frankie" Higdon and his memory. Frankie was more like a brother than a cousin. His remarkable life and his tragic death changed me forever and helped me to realize we only have today to help someone. Frankie, I'm profoundly grateful! God bless you!

DEDICATION

I dedicate this to my mother and father, Freddie and Mary Higdon, who both passed away in 2016. They always taught me to remember where I came from and to never forget who I was. I would have been lost without their guidance, love and courage.

With all my heart, I also dedicate this book to my lovely wife, Kelly, and my three incredible children, Zackary, Jacob and Samantha. You are my life and I love you all!

ABOUT THE AUTHOR

For over two decades as a successful financial planner, Terry Higdon has developed relationships with his clients to build their wealth and to secure their futures using easy to understand strategies with a sincere desire to help people attain their goals. An avid sports enthusiast and coach, Terry knows how to motivate people to make their dreams come true. Terry Higdon is the creator of the highly acclaimed Retirement Made S.I.M.P.L.E.™ Plan that serves as a "Retirement Playbook" for those nearing retirement or already retired.

From an early age, Terry had a passion for helping people. Born into a close-knit, hard-working family, Terry learned never to take anything for granted.

Terry has always had a love for sports and competition. The lessons he learned both on and off the field helped guide him in his professional and personal life. These lessons were the driving force in developing a strategy to create a better awareness and understanding for assisting people in retirement. Terry believes one of the main concepts retirees need to understand is "It's not what you make that is important, but rather what you get to keep". Terry is married to his childhood sweetheart (Kelly) and is the father of three children (Zack, Jake, & Samantha).

TABLE OF CONTENTS

CHAPTER 1

REMEMBER WHERE YOU COME FROM

One of the things I often hear from my clients is that my approach is different from other advisors. I believe that to truly help my clients, I need to understand where they came from. It's important to me to develop an understanding of their past experiences and most important, what their goals are and where they want to end up. Just like I ask of my clients, I wanted to start this book by sharing where I came from.

When I was born in Louisville, Kentucky, the Beatles, and Rolling Stones were at the top of the charts. The TET Offensive in Vietnam occurred, and the U.S. foreign policy changed forever. It was a time when people didn't appreciate the brave men and women who served our great nation. Today, fortunately, our country embraces our veterans as we thank each of them for their service!

I was also born into a year of firsts. Dr. Christian Barnard performed the world's first heart transplant. And the 911 Emergency Phone System was incorporated. It was a big year in sports. The Detroit Tigers played the St. Louis Cardinals. In the Super Bowl, Vince Lombardi's Green Bay Packers defeated the Oakland Raiders!

On a more somber note, the Hong Kong Flu pandemic caused great turmoil, something similar to what we witnessed recently. We've also seen the stock market tank with the Dow hitting 21,679. By comparison, the Dow in 1968 was 943.

Gas was $.34 per gallon. As you can see, times have changed dramatically.

What has not changed is my enthusiasm for sports. Sports have always meant a great deal to me. As an eight-year-old, I won the Best Player Award in the State Little League tournament. I took a lot of pride in achieving that award. I was not a great hitter, but I played a mean defense, making diving catches and strong defensive plays. I worked hard to do my best and the same is true today.

If I do lose a game or contest, I will gladly shake the hand of the winner and tell them, "Great game!" There are always lessons to be learned, even in a loss.

The confidence you get when you attain your goals is amazing. I have always been the kind of guy who wanted the ball in my hands and to take the shot at the buzzer and score! Winning and achieving a goal as part of a team makes it even better. I continue this team approach with my clients today.

Another area that has not changed is that family means the world to me. My parents married young and had me right away. They gave up a great deal to raise me, my sister and my little brother. There was only a seventeen year age difference between myself and my parents. As a matter of fact, many times as I got older, they thought my dad was my brother. The maxim our parents taught us was, "Remember who you are and where you come from." It is excellent advice no matter how you look at. Those words stuck with me my entire life. I'm not saying I didn't kick up my heels a few times with my friends when I got older. I did. Yet, my parents' words have always been in my heart and have guided my life.

My family lived modestly. Dad was in the printing profession and worked long hours just to make ends meet. He'd pick up an extra shift, so we had extra money. Even my mom worked in retail at a store called Bacon's, which is now Dillard's. We learned about the importance of money and not to throw it away. We couldn't. When you think about it, no one should throw money away.

I was raised to help people and to appreciate family and friends. Frequently, we would visit my dad's parents. It was great fun! My dad had five brothers and sisters, who in turn had several kids. Time spent with them was filled with game nights and cards! Our family stuck together, and we always had one another's backs.

To a large extent, our neighbors were also family to us. They were an integral part of our infrastructure, giving us a sense of security. If something happened, there was always someone there to help, no matter what. I've always had trouble asking for help, but it was consoling that there were people in our lives who would help us. But as I said, I prefer to help other people.

Sometimes we would all go camping together. We went to the Daniel Boone State Park, near Winchester, Kentucky, or the Kentucky Horse Park in Lexington, Kentucky. It was a beautiful place with lots to do and lots of history. We had a blast!

On weekends when we were not with our parents, we would go to my grandparents so they could enjoy time with their friends. Come Sunday morning, my grandmother would take us all to church. My faith means a lot to me. I know that God is in control—although sometimes I may feel like I've got the wheel. I learned quickly that God is driving, and I just need to do my best and to help people.

Helping people has always been a great motivator for me. If there's anything I can do for somebody, I'm there. It's just the way I am. Perhaps it is my coach's nature to guide people and support them through the rough spots. I have been blessed to coach sports and to assist in molding young players.

My coaching skills translated into my business life, where helping people as a financial advisor has become my passion. Financial planning is really a team sport and the clients have an integral role in that planning. While I earn a good living at what I do, money is not the driving force behind me. If it were, I would need to find another line of work.

In doing this book, I reflected on the good times and the bad. I had two near death experiences when I was about three years old. They were the kind of incidents that would make your parents age ten years just getting through them. You know, I shouldn't even be here today, and I wouldn't be, if God hadn't watched out for me.

One day, I snuck out of the back yard. I climbed a ladder and got out. I ended up in a swimming pool in the deep end. My grandmother came out of the house and looked around the backyard.

"Where's Terry?" she asked, concerned.

My Uncle Frankie got out and went to look for me. He found me in the pool and pulled me out by my hair. I barely made it.

Another time I almost did not make it was when I climbed up and got a bottle of isopropyl rubbing alcohol from the bathroom counter. I drank it! The doctors didn't think I'd make it. They pumped my stomach, but they still didn't have a positive prognosis. My poor mother was scared to death. When I did survive, thank God, the doctor told my mom I was a fighter. I guess I am.

My dad and I had a great deal in common. We really were alike in most things. Sometimes that was good and then at times, it was not. As I got older, the competitive sports-minded nature I inherited from my dad continued. Sometimes, we had arguments that would erupt into heated situations. Competitive, neither of us would give in. When two people are that much alike, it can make life difficult, especially with two alpha males.

My mom was the sweetest woman in the world. Everyone who met her thought the same thing. She was such a wonderful, loving woman. One day, my mom suggested that I move out on my own. Afterall, I was eighteen and could move out. I saw her point and to keep peace in the house, I decided to go. I was faced with having to find my own place, to get a job and to figure out how to go to college at the same time.

Lessons about money were learned quickly. You get a new perspective on things when you're the one paying the bills! I took to my new responsibilities and did well. I had confidence in my own ability and if a mistake was made, I learned from them and moved forward.

For a while, I worked at the printing company where my dad worked. It really wasn't something I liked. I couldn't see myself there and couldn't imagine how my dad worked there for so many years. He didn't seem happy with his job and I couldn't see my future there at all. When an opportunity arose that exposed me to a different profession, I jumped at it.

By this time, I was married and wanted to carve out something new, career wise. I went with my wife Kelly's brother, Ski, and his friend who worked in the long-term care business, to play in a softball game. I am glad I did!

During the game, we talked about the company that sponsored the softball team. Several of the guys worked there. After the game, the guys asked me to go along with Mike for a week to see if I'd like the work. That was in August 1996, and I'm still in the business today, although, more on the financial side.

I really got hooked when I met with a couple who sent in a request for financial advice. I was based in Louisville, but they were in Cincinnati, which was about an hour and half away. I met with the couple, who were in their late seventies. They truly lived a humble lifestyle. They had an old console television set in the living room at a time when flat screen TVs were the norm. You could tell they needed to watch every penny.

They wanted to discuss healthcare and long-term care, something that at their age was vital. I sold them a policy and upon delivering them the contract, we got to talking about financials. I could tell they didn't have much money.

So, I asked them to find their statements for me so I could help to see if we couldn't find a way to alleviate their financial burden. The wife went to get some documents from her old cedar chest and came back with them.

She put them down on the table. To my utter amazement, there were a bunch of Proctor and Gamble stock certificates!

"What's that about?" I asked. I was very curious.

"Oh, that's just some old company stock from Proctor and Gamble where I used to work," the wife replied, sort of matter-of-fact.

She didn't know what they were sitting on financially!

Even more curious, I said, "Have you guys checked on this? Do you know what the value is for this stock? Has it split?"

"No. We got them, and we threw them in there and forgot about them," the wife said.

I made a few calls to find out more. At the end of the day, we found out the stock was worth $1.5 million dollars! Can you imagine? They had those certificates in their cedar chest for a long time not realizing what they had. They had pinched pennies unaware that a gold mine could be found in their own home!

Upon further investigation, we learned that the stocks were part of an employer stock option and there wouldn't be excessive capital gains from the sale of the stock—a real blessing.

We ended up selling off the stock and putting some of the money into annuities and some other money into cash accounts. To many people a windfall like that would change their lives. They might go on spending sprees, buying cars, houses or going on extended vacations.

Not this couple, they were set in their ways. I mean really set in their ways. Being in their late seventies, they weren't about to change. While the money gave them a sense of security, it didn't blind them or alter their lifestyle.

They told me that if they had found out twenty years before, it might have changed their lives, but not now. Finding out the stocks had true value was a surprise for them. They knew their legacy for their family was established and that made them happy. Their children and grandchildren would live better lives.

True to form, they kept living the way they always had. However, I did convince them to buy a new flat screen TV.

Their story changed my life and gave me a passion for helping people with their financial situation. Had that elderly couple been advised properly, their retirement years would have been easier for them. I want everyone to experience a secure financial future.

Not many of us experience windfalls like that nor do we win the lottery. Their story underscored the necessity to teach people how to take control of their lives and to make sure they made their money work for them. People work hard all their lives just to make ends meet. It's critical that the money you earn works hard for you!

The problem today is that there's a gap in financial education. We tend to go with the flow, to do what our parents did, and their parents and so on. We don't stop to educate ourselves about money. Instead, we watch commercials about the stock market and other investment opportunities without thinking critically about what they're all about.

We put off planning for retirement thinking we'll figure it out when we need to. The time to educate is now, not when retirement is just around the corner.

The internet does provide a means for financial education, but often that education is over our heads. Complicated and time consuming, it's easy to get lost in the hype. In many ways, it's meant to be that way. We are enticed to invest in the market. It's a necessity for brokerage houses to sell the idea to Americans to jump in the market. That's how they stay afloat. It's the fees we pay them that keep them going. Naturally, they're going to tell us to stay in the game.

People can get overwhelmed, but don't worry. That's where I can help. I have broken down the ins and outs of financial education so that you can easily understand what it's all about. Really!

I'll show you how easy it all can be. Your eyes will be opened, and you'll be able to make sound decisions about your financial future. You won't glaze over from all the facts and figures. You won't get lost or buried under the weight of Fuzzy Math that we see so much of today.

I'll show you the easy steps to change your life and provide for a wonderful future. When I had those near-death experiences, I was aware even from an early age that we must make the most of the time we have.

So ... make the most of your life! Join me on this exciting journey into financial security.

Are you ready? Don't worry! It's S.I.M.P.L.E.!

CHAPTER 2

THE "WHAT IF" RETIREMENT

I got into boxing early as a kid. Boxing was natural for me. I liked knowing how to take care of myself. Knowing how to take care of yourself in any given situation is important. It leads to self-confidence.

Bruce Lee and Chuck Norris movies were big at the time. They were awesome and inspired me to be part of the martial arts scene. Fortunately, one of my uncles was in a martial arts class. My uncle encouraged me to come to the class. Intrigued, I went and fell in love with the sport.

I started taking classes and learned to fight with your hands in close-up, tight situations where you can't get off a kick. It was a form of Shaolin Kung Fu, called Lung Shih Po. When you're confronted with someone or something, you need to act quickly and being good with your hands is critical.

I wanted to fight competitively. So, I got into K.I.K.S., which was the Kentucky-Indiana Karate System. I fought in a lot of those competitions.

Martial arts not only train your body, but also your mind. Your mind must be as strong as your body. We are taught meditation and deep breathing exercises that really work.

As a kid, I was entranced with baseball, football and basketball. My dad was my little league coach and he coached me from when I was five until I was fourteen. He taught me that if you want to get a lot out of something, you must put a great deal into it. I was taught the value of teamwork, but I also learned the value of coaching. It was my father's coaching influence that inspired me to become a coach when I grew up.

> LeBron James has a commercial out now for an app called Calm. The tagline is "While the greats train their body, the greatest train their mind."

It's true. We need focus, not just for sports but also for everything we do. We need to train our minds for our retirement as well. We need to bring our financial picture into sharp focus so that we can see where we are headed and the best way to get there.

With plenty of "What Ifs" in life, and particularly in retirement, we need to discern the best approach to realize the results we need. Frequently, people are overwhelmed by all the financial ads about building wealth. Each of those ads come from a different perspective.

Stock Brokerages place their ads on TV and radio and use print ads as well, bombarding us with all sorts of information. Most of us can recall the mantras of those commercials. The slogans easily worm their way into our psyches, programming us with the party line.

We must be careful with the news and do our own homework so that we're not being misinformed. To make informed decisions, we must have the right information. Biased and inaccurate news is changing the way we view the world. That's not conducive to financial planning.

The problem is, does that really help the individual investor? Does it help with the surprises and detours that are found on the way to retirement?

We need to know what the truths are about financial planning. We need to focus and educate ourselves about the options we face.

Commercials inundate us with products and compel us to buy into them. Confusion sets in and we lose our focus, and that can cause us to make bad decisions. Newscasts are no different, often portraying situations in a skewed light.

With all the financial products out there, it's hard to know which ones are best suited for our individual needs. These products are not a One Size Fits All type of thing, even though we're given the impression that they're good for everybody.

I don't talk to clients about products. I find out what my client's goals and needs are and then we focus on getting the necessary results that will secure their futures and their retirement. The product isn't the pertinent key, but rather the tool to getting the optimal results. To help with that discovery process, it's important to look at the possibilities of what could happen on the way to retirement and how to address the hurdles we may encounter. In helping my clients, it's a must to determine their individual goals and needs.

Looking at financial planning, it can be like white water rafting. There can be fast currents, with lots of rocks along the way. It's important to find the right financial advisor who can guide you through the rough water. Two kinds of financial advisors are out there to help.

One kind of advisor will put you in the raft, hand you the oars and point you downstream, while he stands on the shore and waves. The other kind of advisor will not let you go through the rapids alone. Instead, he'll hand you life vests, climb in the boat with you and take the lead. He'll guide you through the turbulent waters of finance. I prefer to be in the boat with my clients. Teamwork is always better!

We also want to make sure that the solutions and products are right for you. You may be directed toward a suitable product by some advisors, but that doesn't mean the product is in your best interest! Just because it's suitable doesn't mean it will work in every situation. It must be right for the individual investor. I make sure I take the time to discover your needs and goals so that the solutions are tailored for your unique circumstances.

THE "WHAT IFS" OF RETIREMENT

Here is a list of some of the "What Ifs" you should consider:

1. What if I live too long?
2. What if I take too much money out of my portfolio?
3. What if there are problems with inflation?
4. What if I go into long-term care?
5. What if I lose money right after I decide to retire?
6. What if I die?

"What Ifs" abound when it comes to retirement planning! Still, they each have one thing in common—longevity! Without a doubt, longevity multiplies the risks.

For instance, the longer you live, the more market swings you'll see. The longer you live, the more you'll encounter inflation and deflation. The longer you live, you will also see more withdrawal rate changes and increase the risk of the sequence of returns affecting you. The longer you live, the more likely it is that you'll need long-term care-Don't worry. We will discuss this later in the book.

> The sequence of returns is the sequential analysis of investment returns. In retirement it can mean a lower than expected rate of return.

> How can you build a secure retirement plan? It's simple. Take longevity out of the equation!

Sounds reasonable, but how do you accomplish that?

The answer is easy:

GUARANTEED INCOME!

Each of us needs an income stream that will be there until we die. It gives us a sense of security and helps us to sleep at night. Just knowing the money is there and will be there month after month, year after year, removes a heavy burden and assures us that we will have the money we need throughout retirement. Many people are in the stock market facing the ups and downs so common with Wall Street. They pay fees and taxes for the privilege.

WHAT IF THE MARKET GOES DOWN?

If the market goes down, one of two things may happen. The investor's lifestyle must change because their money will not last as long. Things like trips, cars and even necessities will tumble off the list. The second thing that can happen is the result of decreased income. A person may have a work-tirement. With the income shortfall, a person would have little choice but to return to work. That's not what retirement is supposed to be!

Is the stock market detrimental to retirement planning? Absolutely!

There are three stages of retirement planning.

Where are you in the retirement planning phase?

1. Accumulation Phase - From 25-49 (Work and Save as much as you can)

2. Preservation Phase - From 50-60 (Not retired, but actually thinking about Retirement, so you move to Safer options in your retirement portfolio)

3. Distribution Phase - From 61-Up (How can I be efficient in getting the most from my Retirement portfolio?)

We have different phases in our life. In our 20s, 30s and 40s we're in the Accumulation Phase. This stage is the time to get enough funds to fuel your retirement. In today's economy, it's best to start early and be disciplined. It's like martial arts, training the mind and becoming disciplined when it comes to our money will protect us from difficult financial situations.

When we enter our 50s and 60s, we are in a new phase called the Distribution Phase. It's the time period when people begin to draw Social Security or withdraw from their 401k.

In our mid-60s, we slide into the Preservation Mode. In this stage, it's essential that we don't lose any money and put our retirement funds in Intensive Care. We don't want that big financial karate blow to knock us down. Even if you retire with enough money, one serious blow can ruin all your plans. A domino effect can hit, and you could find yourself on the ropes.

I see this whole thing like running a race. In every race, we must make it to the finish line! We don't want to fall short. We don't want to become derailed. With retirement, some people run past the finish line.

At some point, you're going to get tired of running. You'll be worn out. When that happens, you'll face all the "What Ifs" of retirement planning. When you have the appropriate plan in place, you have what you need to see things through. You have control of retirement and not the other way around.

Understanding Your Options

As a financial advisor, I talk with people all the time. I ask people to think about this: In America, we insure just about everything.

-  Cars
-  Motorcycles
-  Homes
- 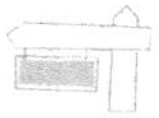 Rental Properties
-  Boats and planes

We insure almost anything of value. But why don't we insure our incomes? I tell people it is possible to ensure your income and to insure where that income comes from. People can ensure that they won't run out of money. If money is our biggest asset, why don't more people insure it? It could be the fact that many people don't know that it's possible. Yet, it is possible, and many people have figured it out and now have peace of mind. You can, too!

I work with my clients to help them determine their goals for retirement by asking questions that go to the heart of the matter. Do they want to travel? If so, how much money do they want to allocate for their travel plans?

Perhaps they want to buy an RV. Well, how much is the RV going to cost? Basically, I help my clients figure out what they'll need to realize their goals and dreams. Once that is established, they know what net amount they'll need each month.

Then we create the income and withhold the taxes on it. Consequently, they have what they need!

When clients come to me, I show them how to handle their liquid assets. I don't recommend they do this or that. I leave the decision up to my clients. But I do advise them of their options. I don't deal in fixed assets; however, should a client sell a house, they suddenly have a liquid asset that we can put into the retirement equation. If they have rental property and are receiving rent, they are making a passive income.

Essentially, there are only three ways of getting a guaranteed income.

- Social Security
- Pensions
- Annuities

Social Security may undergo some changes. We're also seeing that pension funds are dwindling as fewer employers are offering them. If you're working for the government, if you're a teacher or work on the railroad, you'll have a good pension. Private sector employees may not have any pension plans in place.

If you're not in that situation, annuities can be helpful depending on circumstances. A perfect product doesn't exist. That's why finding out my client's needs is pivotal. We can then design the appropriate financial plan to help. If they want to invest in the market, say 30 percent of the money, then we'll put that percentage into the market. However, we will put stop loss measures in place, so my clients aren't hit with a catastrophic loss. I advise my clients about following the Rule of 100. We subtract your age from 100. If you're fifty, 50 percent of your investments should be exposed to risk and in the market. However, if you agree with the Rule, then the other 50 percent should be in Safe strategies without Risk.

I care deeply about my clients and their welfare and never want them to be exposed to more Risk than their acceptable level.

Financial planning is a personal process. You can't pick a plan off the shelf and hope it will work. I thoroughly go over things with my clients, which helps to form a complete picture of their needs.

We determine where things fall on the emotional scale and design a plan that is well-suited for them as individuals. Financial planning is age specific. You don't design the same plan for someone in their 30s and apply that plan to someone in their 60s, or vice versa. We don't design a plan for an eighty-year-old and use that plan for someone in their 60s.

Entering retirement means that time is no longer your ally. Life is entirely different at that stage and you must make the most of it. It's like in a martial arts tournament. You have a set time for rounds. As you age, the time passes more quickly, and you have less time to do something with your money. In my opinion, the only way to make money in the Market is over Time, not timing the Market. Most individuals that try to Time the Market are unsuccessful. That's why the stock market isn't always the best place for your funds when you hit retirement age. There is less time to recoup your funds should there be a drop in the Dow or S&P for example.

I've had clients come to see me after they lost a ton of money in the market. That was especially true when the market fell 40 percent in the 2008 crash.[1] It was even truer during the Covid-19 crisis. The market can look attractive and strong, but is it the best place for your money?

In talking to my clients who've had significant losses, but are once again attracted to the market, we must only take them down memory lane to when they had their big financial loss.

Structuring financial planning based on my client's needs, gives them the foundation they need to succeed and to find peace of mind. They won't need to worry about crashes robbing them of their hard-earned money. My clients can rest easy and I wouldn't have it any other way.

Growth in retirement is not the most important thing. People don't need to incur losses in their retirement years. They need to be assured their money is safe, but they also can make plans to help that fund grow

1 http://www.nbcnews.com/id/37740147/ns/business-stocks_and_economy/t/historic-bear-markets/#.XmKJX6hKiUk

over time. It's not what you Make in Retirement that is important, but what you are allowed to Keep. There is a big difference in those two things, and we will cover more in the upcoming chapters. Financial planning is like stepping into the ring. Taxes, market fluctuations and inflation are your opponents. You must train hard to beat them. You must focus on the important things at hand. You will defeat the foe and not get knocked down.

The unknown can also be a formidable opponent. Like most people don't realize that Social Security is only 100 percent funded until 2034. After that, it's only 80 percent funded.[2] How will that affect you?

A lot of people aren't going to get the benefits they thought they were. That adds a new element that must be handled ahead of the change.

Our mindset needs to change when we hit retirement. We must look at things differently to prepare and to survive. I use case studies to help my clients see the big picture.

For example, a personal case study I often reference is

2 https://blog.ssa.gov/social-security-funded-until-2034-and-about-three-quarters-funded-for-the-long-term-many-options-to-address-the-long-term-shortfall/

from when my grandmother was sick, and my mother needed to take care of her. When my grandmother made my mother promise she would not be put into a nursing home, that placed a great deal of pressure and stress on my mother. Certainly, my grandmother needed care, so much so that my mother suffered for it. The thing was that my grandmother dropped her long-term care coverage because she didn't want to pay the increase to her premium, which was about $130 more per year. In the end, that decision impacted my mother and her health. She developed early onset Alzheimer's. Had my grandmother known that would happen, she never would have insisted that my mother make that promise.

Planning is key to a healthy retirement where you can have enough money to meet your needs and I can help.

Here's a question for you? What does your ideal retirement look like? If you're unsure, no worries. The next chapter will help you figure that out!

CHAPTER 3

WHAT DOES YOUR RETIREMENT LOOK LIKE?

My boys and I were shooting our weekly video and we got to a stopping point and decided to go to Chick-Fil-A to have some lunch. After lunch, we headed out and I went to my car, a carry-out bag in hand for my wife and daughter.

It was a sunny day. So, I stopped and put on my sunglasses to block the glare. I saw what I thought was my silver SUV. As I got closer, I saw a big old scratch on the door. Immediately, I thought someone hit my SUV. Noticing the color of paint on the door, I looked around the parking lot to see if any of the cars in the area were the same color. They weren't.

I thought that the person in the other vehicle must have left before I got out to the lot. My focus turned quickly to the scratch. Now, this might seem gross to you, but I licked my fingers thinking I might rub some of the paint off. Growing up without much, we learned to appreciate everything we had. Consequently, I learned to take care of my things. My SUV was no exception.

Rubbing on the scratch, I tried my best to remove the paint. When it wouldn't rub off, I began to think about the bodywork that needed to be done. I was frustrated now. Determined to rub out the scratch, I put the carry out bags down and continued to rub the scratch. I didn't realize my son was in his car right behind me. He honked the horn.

I turned and looked at him. He was laughing hard.

"Dad, that's not your car," he exclaimed, still laughing.

"What do you mean?"

"You parked down there," my son replied.

And I looked and there was my vehicle a little further away. Now, my wife, Kelly, will tell you I normally don't do things like that. I'm a very analytical guy. I reason things out from every possible angle. Making mistakes like that just doesn't happen to me. I keep track of things. Totally aware of my surroundings, I keep my bearings. That day, I mixed up the cars. Unfortunately, for the real owner, they had expensive work to get done on the car. I was blessed it wasn't mine.

This story points out that in our busy world with so much on our minds, it's easy to get confused. That certainly relates to retirement planning. Another prime example of how busy and distracted we are can be found in the yield sign.

Do you know what color a yield sign is?

For decades, the yield sign was yellow. Now, it's red and white. Have you noticed that? If you haven't, you're not alone. We don't pay attention to things the way we should.

> Caught up in our busy schedules, we don't think we have the time to research our investment opportunities, often putting off decisions that should be made while we're in the accumulating stage of our lives.

In planning for retirement, we need to have an "I Know So" source of income, not an "I Hope So." We need to have the assurances that if the market goes down, we are covered. No one wants to suffer losses in financial planning. By having a guaranteed source of income, we eliminate the risk and negate the need to change our lifestyles. That's why getting to know my clients is so important. Cookie cutter approaches don't work when it comes to planning for retirement. Every case is different and should be treated as such.

With a guaranteed income, you'll have peace of mind. The happiest people in retirement are police officers, firemen, teachers, and government workers. They have guaranteed income for the rest of their lives. It's the maximum safety net for retirement and a must have in your retirement planning tool kit.

People who live day to day hoping to get by live life on a tightrope, a precarious place to be. When the winds of change blow hard, like in a stock market crash, you could lose 50 percent of your investments in a heartbeat. Stress like that will rob you of sleep and peace of mind.

There's no reason to stress out when you can make positive changes in your income and retirement picture.

Hitting the right income mark for your lifestyle is essential to ensuring your future.

> Ask yourself this question: Are you trying to hit a home run and become rich in retirement or do you just not want to be poor and have enough money to meet your needs and continue to live a comfortable lifestyle?

Getting the guaranteed income amount right in retirement planning is pivotal to a happy retirement. During your whole life, you're going to do two things. You are either going to give your money away or you're going to spend it, as Tom Hegna would say.

If you don't spend your money, I guarantee your kids will. Kids often see inheritance as a windfall and they're quick to buy the new car or house they set their hearts on. They won't think about the future and the need for money down the road. It's like winning the lottery.

We hear so much about bucket lists, the things we'd like to do while we're on earth. If you don't live your bucket list, your kids will live it for you. Figuring out what you want to do with your money ahead of time will help you to make the best decisions for you and your family. What we decide today can impact our families for years to come.

If you plan on a big vacation and don't take it, your kids will take it after you're gone. Realizing what you want to do now will help you in the future. I want people to enjoy their hard-earned money now. It's important to me they understand how, and it should be important to you because you have worked too hard.

You worked a lifetime accumulating funds that will help you to retire. Kids may easily go through all the money you leave them within two or three years. Taking stock of your needs and desires now will help you to see the path you need to take to achieve security.

If you want to retire and have a guaranteed income and still leave a financial legacy to your children, set up a distribution schedule of that inheritance so that it's not blown all at once. It perpetuates the family legacy while preserving funds for the future. If done properly, it could be a solid legacy for future generations.

The guru of financial success, Warren Buffett has wonderful words of wisdom that will help you when it comes to leaving your children a legacy.

> Leave your children, "enough money so that they would feel they could do anything, but not so much that they could do nothing."
>
> – *Warren Buffett*

ALLEVIATING ANXIETY IN RETIREMENT

People tend to put off retirement planning and before they realize it, retirement is just around the corner. Life passes quickly and sometimes we are ill-prepared. Most people need to feel that things are going to be okay. No matter what, they want to be reassured that they will be taken care of. It's my job and privilege to help them with that. I do reassure my clients that they'll be okay and set up a plan that will give them the reassurance, and more importantly, peace of mind that it will work out for them.

For example, people faced with early retirement from their employers can be thrown into a quandary about what to do.

We can sit down and work through that and find the very best solutions for that person's individual circumstances.

Recently, I had a couple come into my office seeking advice. The husband was offered a buyout from a carmaker that could greatly impact his retirement plan. He asked me what he should do. I reminded him to remember his goals. Ultimately, you have to decide on the things that are important to you and your family.

I then coached him through all of his options. We went through the numbers and looked at the tax situation and different scenarios so that he could make an informed decision. If he wanted to roll the money over into a Roth IRA, we could look at that, too.

> Roth IRA's work well if you suspect your taxes will be higher.

We should look at that. So, we went through the different scenarios to see all the variables.

The man could use the cash from the buyout and open a joint account along with various options. The man had a lot of questions. I could tell he was worried about what to do.

"Should I take a lump sum? Should I take the monthly income payout where I'm getting 100 percent of the benefit, but if I die, my wife will only get 65 percent? And what about if I die and my wife gets 100 percent of the benefit, but that means we would take less income now?"

All were valid and important questions. When we are faced with important financial decisions, we can easily get overwhelmed when there are so many options. Well, I ran through the numbers with them and

I could tell there was a sense of relief. They already knew what they wanted their retirement to look like. Having that vision established, they could make the best decision based on the numbers and what was right for them.

I analyze each client's needs individually. We'll run the numbers to see if they'll be okay. We'll look at things from every possible angle to ensure they will indeed be fine. Looking at the numbers and asking the right questions help us to determine the client's comfort zone.

Can you live on $5000 per month and have enough to meet your needs? What about $4000 per month? Breaking things down to the least common denominator, discovering the client's expenses and their needs, and applying income scenarios, we can say with assurance, "Yes, you will be okay!" We want to define the magic income number that will help the client say, "Yes, we can live on that!"

Living your normal lifestyle and being comfortable is important. Together, we will find that comfort zone and make sure it's sustainable. Each of us has 168 hours per week to spend. How you spend those hours in retirement is determined by your income.

During our working years, it's a no-brainer. We get up

to go to work Monday through Friday. We're working to acquire the funds we'll need for retirement. However, when we hit retirement, life changes. Every day is Saturday! We wake up and figure out what we're going to do today. Saturday's are more laid back. We go with the flow and take it easy. We think about if we're going to go shopping, see a movie or take a trip. Maybe we'll eat out or have friends over. Basically, in retirement, we figure out what we're going to spend our money on today. While in our working years, our Accumulating Years, we're trying to save as much money as possible, at least that should be our goal.

Establishing a plan, and having parameters set in place means you will have the confidence and reassurance that you will be okay! It's even better to formulate that plan early. Your goals are established without last minute preparation and you're more prepared to meet those goals in retirement.

Breaking down the numbers with my clients usually results in a light bulb turning on for them. I can see it in their eyes. They get it! They understand the facts and they can now plan. They feel in control. That's something everyone needs to feel.

> Keep control of your life and your money!

The confidence a person gets when they've acquired the knowledge they need is invaluable.

> I love to see the light bulb light up in my clients!

Helping people is what I love to do. Doing the right thing is extremely important to me. I have to know I've done my very best to help people. That's what it's all about, isn't it?

There are a lot of people out there today that spin the coverage for clients giving them the impression they are getting one thing but really, they are getting something else. People do not read the fine print of the verbose contracts, which most of the time are written in legalese. They can be difficult to understand and interrupted in many ways.

For example, recently there was a merger between a local hospital and a local university. The merger caused confusion for the employees. Being two large institutions, the ripple effects went through the community. People were concerned about being taxed on their money. Would they have to roll over the money into a new 401k? Rumors were swirling all over the place! That alone added to the confusion and anxiety.

One of my current clients spoke with her sister, who was employed by the hospital. She decided to come and see me. After creating a plan for her situation, she referred two other women from her unit.

Long story short, we were able to help all of the clients who came in to see us. They were so happy, they passed my name on to family and friends. People know that I'm there for them. Whatever they need, I'm there. Even if we don't end up doing business, we part as friends. We're all in this together and helping each other is the best way to go through life!

The best way to help people is to establish their goals, to listen, and to learn about their vision for retirement. I've said before, it's not about the product. It's reaching the goals. There are a lot of products out there than are considered suitable. They're registered in the state where they're sold. Suitability, however, doesn't mean the product is going to be in your best interest.

Take IRAs and 401ks for instance. Many people don't know you have more options within an IRA than you do with a 401k.

Here's an analogy on the 401k:

Let's say you walk into a grocery store with forty

aisles. You walk around the store and find out that you can only enter four of those aisles. The rest of the thirty-six aisles are blocked off. If you take control of your assets and move them into a personal IRA, suddenly, all forty aisles are open to you! It makes the decision process simple!

We can still leave your 401k open, and that's a good idea especially if you're getting matching funds. We won't close the 401k, but we're moving your vested balance into the IRA where you have more control of your money. We always look for solutions with your best interest in mind!

Having been involved in sports, one way or another most of my life, I believe in the team effort when it comes to achieving goals. Not all advisors believe that. Not all advisors listen.

CASE IN POINT

A man, let's call him Walter, went in to see a financial planner. He wanted to invest some money, and the planner was happy to assist him. Yet, the planner never asked him if he would need to touch the money at some future date or what he intended to use the money for. Walter had a lump sum distribution and it was taken at that. He had plans on buying a house in

Florida within a couple of years. To his surprise, the planner locked him into a seven-year product. Walter wouldn't be able to access his funds and consequently, buying the home in Florida wouldn't be possible. His money was tied up.

Initially, Walter stated he wanted his money to be secure, but when the planner failed to find out his goals, he did Walter a huge disservice. To get his money out, he would have fourteen years of surrender charges, a heavy price to pay for the planner's insufficient client research and his failure to fully disclose the product parameters.

Well, we started writing letters on his behalf. Yes, Walter signed all the contracts, but we stated the man never got an explanation of the terms and the conditions of the contract. If this case ever went to court, the seller of the product would end up in a bad light. Most companies don't want to go there. The companies will normally capitulate and return the money.

The reason we ask so many questions of our clients is to gain all the information we can. Then we know exactly what they want, their goals and expectations. We make sure that the client knows all the ins and outs of where they're putting their money. It's the ethical thing to do.

Doing due diligence and getting to know your client will help the client to reach their goals. It's honest and it's simple. I love to break things down for my clients so that everything is understood and there are no questions and surprises.

In the next chapter, we'll break things down and introduce you to the S.I.M.P.L.E. Plan. It's a game changer!

CHAPTER 4

"S" IS FOR SOCIAL SECURITY

We're going to look at the S.I.M.P.L.E.™ Plan that will make your life easier and your retirement the very best it could be. Your retirement will be a place where your income and your lifestyle are secure. We will show you the roadmap to peace of mind. After years of hard work, retirement is the time you should enjoy, not something to worry about.

Breaking it down, step-by-step, you will see what your retirement will look like if you follow the plan. As a coach, I want to inspire you, to motivate you and to help you in your financial planning. So, let's look at "S" for Social Security—the first step in your retirement plan.

We mentioned before having a guaranteed income in retirement is key for your future. Essentially, retirement planning begins with Social Security. Knowing what your benefit will be each month will help determine how to fill any income gap in your retirement plan. Social Security is there every month, the guaranteed income that will be the foundation you can build on.

In doing my workshops, I give people an example. I point out that for some in the audience, Social Security is their biggest asset and they don't even realize it. The crowd laughs. Some people think it's silly that I would say that because I don't know them. They'll respond that Social Security is not their biggest asset.

Some people only get $2000 each month in Social Security. Then I ask the crowd if they know the withdrawal rate. When no one raises their hand, I tell them, "No wonder you're concerned about retirement!"

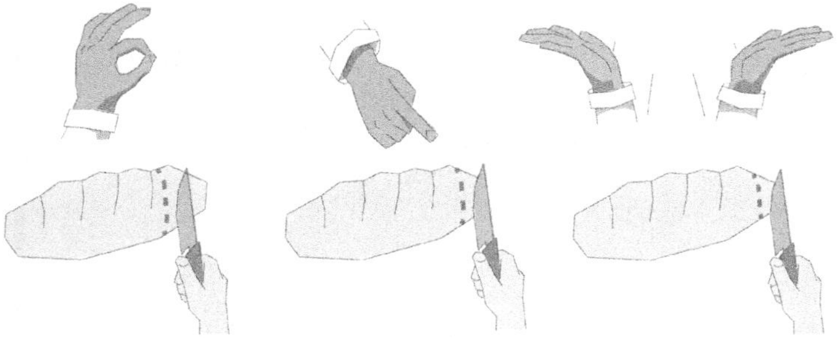

Then I proceed to tell them a story. Many years ago, financial gurus decided that the normal withdrawal rate would be 8 percent when you reach your full retirement age or FRA. In other words, if you save $100,000, you can withdraw $8000 per year without worrying about running out of money. That sounds okay, right? Well, not exactly.

Lo and behold, the gurus found out that the 8 percent withdrawal rate didn't prove to be true because people were running out of money—a scary thought! The gurus rethought the process and decided that the normal withdrawal rate would be 6 percent. If you saved $100,000, you should be able to withdraw $6000 per year and not run out of money.

Then can you guess what happened? You got it! The gurus got together and said, "No, that's not right either!" The rate of withdrawal or return should be 4 percent and that's where it's pretty much stayed. It's what the industry standard average is. However, in October of 2019, Morningstar, the number one third party researcher, announced that 4 percent withdrawal rate isn't right either.[3]

3 https://www.morningstar.com/articles/844210/retirees-are-you-spending-too-much

WHAT IS THE CORRECT AVERAGE WITHDRAWAL RATE?

> Morningstar said the right withdrawal rate was 2.7 percent! Now, if you saved $1 million, you could withdraw $27,000 per year without running out of money.

That's the *most* you can withdraw! Most of the Monte Carlo simulations calculate that this is estimated on a twenty-five to thirty-year payout.

Well, people are living a lot longer. For now, let's look at the 4 percent withdrawal rate for Social Security. If we have a husband and wife and each brings in $20,000, they're bringing in $40,000 per year in Social Security benefits.

Using that 4 percent withdrawal rate, I'll ask the people at my workshops this question:

> How much money would you have in Social Security to fund that income?

People usually don't have an answer. To save time, I'll tell them $1 million! Remember, the withdrawal rate is 4 percent and that's $40,000. Do you have $1 million dollars in Social Security?

Today, people are drawing Social Security randomly without knowing the rules and regulations. This is where things get problematic. People don't know the real value Social Security has in their retirement plan and they don't understand the withdrawal rate. Social Security *can* be an asset.

Many financial advisors encourage their clients to withdraw Social Security at age sixty-two thinking that a bird in the hand is worth more and because you never know when you're going to die. Well, if you're a single person and you need the money, then go ahead and take it. You've got to put food on the table.

However, if you're married, it is almost never a good idea to withdraw Social Security early because there is a high probability one of you will outlive the other. If the higher wage earner withdraws Social Security early, then the spouse would get the lower amount for the rest of their life, should the higher earner die.

> If you take your benefit at sixty-two, you're only receiving 75 percent of what is called your FRA or Full Retirement Age benefits.

If you defer that benefit, now you get the cost of living adjustments. Every year you defer your benefits, you're earning 8 percent simple interest. Adding the cost of living adjustment, for example 2 percent per year, you're now making 10 percent!

Banks aren't offering interest rates that high. Your Social Security asset is much more than you think it is! If you defer the money and don't draw it, you make that 10 percent tax free!

The reason some advisors want you to draw Social Security at an earlier age is because they don't want you to withdraw your money from other investments lowering their commissions or their AUM, Assets Under Management.

Social Security Maximization Analysis

When people come into my office, we run an actual Social Security Maximization Analysis. Then you can figure out what works best for your family's needs. We run this analysis for every client who hasn't started to draw Social Security. Becoming and staying informed is a sound approach in retirement planning.

We want people to see the numbers if they turn on Social Security early or wait ten years and turn it on later. The more you know, the better decisions you'll make for you and your family.

We'll even look at the prospects if you live ten years longer than you expect or die ten years earlier. Looking at those various scenarios, clients get a clearer picture of what to expect.

Today we tend to take Social Security for granted. It's been around all our lives. Yet, it's prudent to take an historical look at Social Security to get a clearer picture of where we are today. When Social Security was first established in 1935, the average life expectancy was fifty-nine or sixty-one.[4] The government thought it had things figured out. People would pay into Social Security and the general fund would not be put into jeopardy because of the average life expectancy at the time. In its wildest dreams, the government never anticipated that people would be living into their eighties and nineties.

Obviously, the need to draw on retirement benefits will be extended.

> ⚠ In the next ten years, projections indicate that for every two people drawing Social Security, only one person is paying in.

That will cause a deficit to occur and problems will arise.

According to the Social Security Administration, in its report "The Future Financial Status of the Social Security Program," they state that by 2037, the Social Security Fund will be exhausted. Those funds are kept in a Trust Account. Social Security Disability funds are

4 https://www.ssa.gov/history/lifeexpect.html or https://web.stanford.edu/class/e297c/poverty_prejudice/soc_sec/hsocialsec.htm

kept in a separate account as well as Medicare. None of these funds can borrow money to replenish the funds should they be exhausted. They must rely on deposits from workers and any government support to sustain the funds.

With people living longer and fewer workers contributing to the fund, it's clear changes must be made. Increasing the retirement age is something that can happen with a stroke of a pen. The government can do what it wants.

My concern is for my clients and their benefits. We lay out the numbers for my clients so they can make smart choices about their Social Security benefits. When we discuss the pros and cons, my clients get a better idea concerning Social Security. It can be a big asset to them and one that will help support their retirement.

I firmly believe the government will do what it takes to keep Social Security funded. Your monthly Social Security benefit will be a lifelong income, something upon which you can depend.

The next step in determining when to turn on Social Security is to evaluate the client's needs. Since I don't know my client's asset structure, it's important to ask specific questions.

What does the client need to live on? Will the client need $3000 or $4000 dollars per month? The average person gets a monthly Social Security benefit of $2000. Therefore, it's necessary to look at other guaranteed income potential. If you don't make enough in Social Security, that means a person would have to tap their nest egg or investments to bridge the gap.

Let's say you need that $3000 per month. Do you take Social Security at sixty-two or do you defer it? Well, if you only have $50,000 saved in other accounts, you're going to want to turn on Social Security sooner to keep your nest egg from being gobbled up.

What if you have saved $300,000? What do you do then?

You would have the option of deferring benefits for a couple of years living off your savings. It's not exactly a guaranteed thing. Still, if you defer taking benefits, your Social Security account is earning 10 percent tax free interest.

Some people will have their money in CDs earning 1 percent annually and go ahead and turn on Social Security early. In my opinion, this is not a sound financial decision.

For instance, if I offered you the choice between $10 or $1, which would you take? Everyone would certainly pick the $10. Although, I've had some people tell me they'd take both! Now, if everybody would take the $10, think about why we would even think about turning on Social Security early if we didn't absolutely need to?

In our younger years—twenties, thirties and forties—we are in the accumulating phase where it's necessary to save, save and then save! It is possible to take on some risks during this phase but that will change as we age.

During the preservation stage, fifty to sixty, we can take some of the money off the table. At this phase, we're now looking at retirement becoming a reality soon and our perspective changes, as it should.

Hitting age sixty-one, we start to think about Social Security and perhaps early retirement. We hear some of our friends who talk about retiring at age sixty-two and drawing their Social Security. Assessing our needs and looking at how much we put into Social Security in our lives, we try to figure out if we are going to have enough to live on and if there is going to be an income gap.

It's my job to help people in their assessment of Social Security and to determine if there will indeed be an income gap. It's also my job, one I take seriously, to help people bridge any gap that may be present. We coach and advise our clients on the best approach, making sure their needs are met with guaranteed income.

We touched on "work-tirement" in a previous chapter. Going back to work has become a trend. I'm seeing a lot of people who have gone back to work before they came to talk with us about their situation.

The AARP cites 54.7 percent of people between the ages of sixty to sixty-four are working at least part time.[5] That's significant! Working may impact your benefits temporarily if you make too much money.

---

5 https://www.aarp.org/research/topics/economics/info-2017/2017-retirement-security-national-survey.html
https://www.ssa.gov/pubs/EN-05-10069.pdf

In the long run, though, your Social Security account will be better because you're paying more money into it.

WHAT ARE THE DRAWBACKS FOR GOING BACK TO WORK UNDER AGE SIXTY-SIX?

Okay, so you may have to fill your income gap by going back to work. How much can you make on Social Security before taxes become an issue?

As of January 2020, you can make the earnings limit of $18,240 if you're under age sixty-six.[6] Remember, you can't confuse earnings limits with taxation on Social Security because they're apples and oranges. It's easy to get the two mixed up.

Should you exceed the earnings limit, for every $2 you make over the limit, $1 is deducted. So, think about whether you should defer your payments.

On the other hand, if you're over age sixty-six, and hit your FRA or Full Retirement Age, you no longer have to worry about income limits.

6 https://www.thebalance.com/how-does-the-social-security-earnings-limit-work-2388828

The increase in retirees going back to work is directly correlated to the fact they didn't have a plan in place to guarantee their income after retirement. We discuss these things in our workshops and give people the tools they need to formulate a plan and maintain their lifestyles with guaranteed income.

If people haven't saved during their working years, it's going to be a problem at retirement because there's little we can do. You can't squeeze blood out of a turnip. A dollar only has one hundred pennies. That's it.

SOMETHING NEW ON THE HORIZON

The Secure Act was signed January 1, 2020 and deals with retirement enhancement.[7] The act touches upon deferring RMDs, Retirement Minimum Distribution, and looking at the new age of seventy-two. If you're still working after age seventy-two, and you can prove your income, you may continue to contribute to your IRA.

The Secure Act also changes how distributions and 401k plans are being handled and setup. Now, annuities will be allowed to be part of that equation.

7 https://www.congress.gov/bill/116th-congress/house-bill/1994

Retirement planning isn't about how much money you make. It's about how much money you get to keep! Our workshops and one-on-one sessions are designed to maximize your bottom line.

Other elements can dramatically hit your bottom line. Things like healthcare costs, and rising Medicare premiums can offset the cost of living increases in Social Security and inflation.

It's our goal to help you achieve financial homeostasis, a place where you're comfortable. Sometimes, people have an abundance of money and while that may seem like a terrific problem to have, it can have its downsides.

Recently, one guy came into my office with a problem. He was making too much money and it was placing him in a higher tax bracket, not a place you want to be. I asked him a question:

"What solutions has your advisor offered you to resolve the issue?"

"He told me to keep doing what I'm doing."

"How does that sit with you?"

"That's why I'm sitting in your office right now."

I'd be sitting there, too, if I'd gotten that advice. Really, that's no advice at all! (We will cover more on personal taxes in a later chapter.)

When asked about my best-case scenario, I thought about the File and Suspend option with Social Security. When that was in force, it was nothing for a person to go from $150,000 to $300,000 in their account given their life expectancy.

Unfortunately, that's not the case now. Due to the Bi-Partisan Act passed on May 1, 2016, that changed. It was the largest reduction in Social Security history and the worst part of all was that people didn't realize it![8]

It's important today to know the rules and regulations involving Social Security and to be creative in your financial planning.

Still, a new strategy is in play and it's one where I recently saved a client $200,000 by using the File and Restrict strategy. If you haven't received twelve full payments on your Social Security, you can still take advantage of the File and Restrict.

---

8 https://www.cbpp.org/research/social-security/more-cuts-to-social-security-administration-funding-would-further-degrade

> The restricted application is a planning tool, used at full retirement age, that allows you to restrict your application for spousal benefits only and delay your own retirement benefit to age 70. This allows you to accumulate delayed retirement credits, effectively increasing your retirement benefit up to 32%.
>
> – *Forbes Magazine*

A woman came into my office after she had received her eleventh Social Security check. With just two days to go, the woman discovered how much she would save by using the old File and Suspend Strategy. She immediately stopped her payments and her husband did, too! After all was said and done, they're saving $300,000!

As people reach retirement age and are ready to draw Social Security, problems can arise depending on relationships. Due to the high number of divorces in our country, and tough economic times, people don't know if remarrying after a divorce will have a negative or positive impact on their Social Security payments. Single women can experience greater hardships as they reach sixty-two.

Many don't realize that if they were married for ten years, they are entitled to their ex-husbands Social Security if they haven't remarried. This can be quite helpful for people in need of more guaranteed income. That benefit doesn't affect the account of the former spouse. Even if you were married to another spouse for ten years, you could choose which spouse was the highest wage earner and draw on that account. The downside is that if you remarried, you're not entitled to those benefits. Just knowing you have options if you're single and close to retirement can help in your overall planning.

In our work, we have been able to save divorcees and people that did not know they could file on their ex-spouses account.

People aren't getting the information they need. When they check the Social Security Handbook, they find that Social Security does not give advice about when to draw and what options are available. The book encourages people to seek sound financial advice. They know the answers, but they're not allowed under law to divulge them.

It pays to educate yourself and to incorporate the very best strategies for your situation. I can help with those strategies!

In the next chapter, we'll move on to the "I" in S.I.M.P.L.E. Plan – Income Planning!

CHAPTER 5

"I" IS FOR INCOME

We have discussed the necessity for having a guaranteed income in retirement. Americans insure just about everything in their lives, but we seldom, if ever, insure our incomes. Having the right income in retirement guarantees that you have a paycheck and a play check, as Tom Hegna would say! You've worked hard all your life and saved money for your retirement.

Our lives can change in a heartbeat, though. The best thing we can do is to plan for the contingencies and the unexpected.

A couple came to one of my Retirement Workshops and they were interested and motivated to learn more about what they could do to prepare for retirement. The husband was the kind of guy who took care of everything, from their money to wills. His wife wasn't involved in the process. They went through the fact-finding stage and then they became clients.

When couples come in, it's always my goal to have them both involved with Retirement and Estate Planning. It's critical. Should one of the spouses die, it's necessary for the surviving spouse to be well-informed about their finances. It can be very hard to make decisions immediately following the death of a loved one.

I showed the couple how they could live on a pre-determined amount of income. They thought they would be fine on $4000 per month. Both were happy with that. We put together their investment plan and the couple was in good shape

Returning home, they began to have some doubts. The "What Ifs" crept in.

What if they got sick? What if that illness required more medications or expensive medications? Oh, and what if something else happens? Things *do* happen. It's part of life.

> Many of us without a solid retirement plan let the "What Ifs" wear us down.

Worry sets in. Doubt follows shortly thereafter and before you know it, fear shows up. It's the troublesome trio. Then the couple thought about the possibilities of long-term care. "What If" that came about? All these questions can impact your decisions.

> That's the reason for the S.I.M.P.L.E.™ Plan. It works. It alleviates doubt, fosters security and peace of mind.

After talking it over, the husband, who was a pharmacist, and the wife who was a nurse, thought they might need extra money. A decision was made to continue working not only because of the "What Ifs" but also, they wanted to travel more.

Sadly, within a short period of time, the husband died of a brain aneurysm. Their plans for retirement together were lost. No one knows the future. We make our decisions based on the information we have.

There was a silver lining to this story, we had gone through the process with both of them. She learned all about finances, retirement planning, and estate planning. She knew where everything was and was prepared to go forward. Basically, she was given an I Love You Will or a Kiss Me Will, a last love letter from her husband. Today, his wife is one of our biggest supporters and never hesitates to recommend people to us.

In retirement planning, income is the key to a successful and strong plan and future. To be secure, you must know where your income is going to come from, how much it is and if it's guaranteed. Life is full of surprises. Retirement isn't the time for financial shocks. It is the time to enjoy life and the money you worked so hard to obtain.

Most people in their early years save and sacrifice so that their families will be all right. By the time a person retires, it's okay to be a little selfish, to spend the money you worked so hard to accumulate and to live the life you want to live.

Having security in our retirement years is worth an awful lot. There's no substitute for peace of mind. If we have a solid plan in place, we're much better off.

We're witnessing many events in this country and the world right now. The ripple effect of wars, diseases, along with stock market ups and downs, political upheavals, inflation and uncertain times can become significant challenges to overcome. Many retirees and pre-retirees are anxious during those challenges.

Why?

The answer is simple! They don't have Guaranteed Lifetime Income.

Look at this historically. Prior to 1984, more than 80 percent of Americans had pensions. Those people had comfort and peace of mind. They could never outlive their money. Imagine that!

Today, how many people have pensions?

The answer might surprise you. It's about 20 percent.[9] It's no wonder that many retirees are concerned about outliving their money.[10]

Essentially, we are placed in the position of making decisions about how long we are going to live, how

9 https://www.pensionrights.org/publications/statistic/how-many-american-workers-participate-workplace-retirement-plans

10 https://www.pensionrights.org/publications/statistic/how-many-american-workers-participate-workplace-retirement-plans

much you can withdraw from your portfolio and how much risk you can afford to take. That's a daunting task for anyone who doesn't understand the Retirement Options available today.

WHY IS GUARANTEED LIFE INCOME SO IMPORTANT?

Guaranteed Life Income is something tangible and something you can spend. Assets are just a bunch of numbers on a piece of paper. With assets can come liens, divorce, lawsuits, losses in the market and so forth.

> Income, on the other hand, is a tangible asset that makes you feel terrific every month when a new check is sent.

Studies have shown that the happiest people in retirement are fire-fighters, police, teachers and government employees. Why are they the happiest? They have no fear of running out of money. Therefore, they can enjoy their retirement to its fullest.

Did you know that people with Guaranteed Income live longer because they don't have the stress and/or worry about their money? It's also true that happy people have fewer physical ailments. People who have steady incomes live happier and healthy lives. Remember, you will do one of two things with your money—you will either spend it or give it. (Tom Hegna)

Most retirees want to spend their money in retirement and then leave what is left to their heirs. Then what's the problem? People don't know how to do it!

Now you see why the proprietary process of the S.I.M.P.L.E. ™ Plan is vital! It illustrates the step-by-step procedures to ensure your Income Stream for life.

Keeping your same lifestyle and the ability to achieve your goals come down to one thing—Income! We want to make sure we get your income right and adjust it for inflation. Getting a pay raise every year is paramount. It helps you stay ahead of inflation and those little or not so little surprises that may appear. Our largest asset is our income and we don't want it to diminish, but rather guarantee it for our lifetime.

Brokers can use analogies and Monte Carlo simulations, which try to predict the probability of outcomes, and those things don't always lead to a feeling of security for clients. They are using assumed interest rates over a specific period. I don't know about you, but I don't like to assume anything! These methods don't guarantee income.

> It's guaranteed income that will make the difference in retirement, not assumptions.

We've long passed the stage of making assumptions. Today, they're not feasible.

SO HOW DO WE GUARANTEE INCOME?

The only way to guarantee income is with an annuity. Math and science support this statement. Many professionals agree that basic needs and longevity expenses must be covered with guaranteed income. The problem is that most people do not understand annuities. Annuities have been around since the days of the Roman army. To fund their wars, they went to towns and asked for money so they could fight. They in turn promised the citizens a future payment.

Well, annuities today are much better than back then. Still, the principle is the same.

If you look on the back of a dollar bill, you'll see the word annuit. It's a promise that you have a $1 of purchasing power, whatever the value of the dollar is at the time.

Like any good coach, it's my goal to motivate you and to ensure your money is always there for you. When crossing the finish line at retirement, you don't need to keep running. You've already finished the race. Yet, some people keep on running, like that couple I mentioned earlier.

People don't know that if they relocate their assets, from one vehicle to another, they're not losing money. It's just repositioning it to do the most good, somewhat like moving money from one pocket to another.

Maximizing your Social Security to its fullest benefits and getting annuities to guarantee income (annuities aren't known for hedging inflation) and growing your money as a hedge against inflation are the best ways to secure your future. The problem is not that people don't listen. It's not your fault! A lot of white noise gets in a person's way. They get distracted with ads from other institutions wanting them to play the game in the market for the "I Hope So" Retirement. It's hard for them to hear the message and to digest it. They need to be reminded the process does not have to be difficult. This is why we created the S.I.M.P.L.E. ™ plan.

Perhaps the quickest way for people to come around is when they're getting close to retirement age and they know they're not going to have steady paychecks coming in. Trepidation sets in. It's then that people finally realize they must create their own paychecks. In a way, the person can become their own banker. Who better to control your money than you? If you don't tell your money what to do, then it will tell you what to do!

We talked earlier about deferring Social Security to your advantage. Just waiting a few years can make a big difference. The same is true with annuities. If you go ahead and buy your annuity but don't draw on it for a few years, it's worth more. That's the point where you don't need to draw on your other assets for income.

It's funny. We're seeing a trend in our office. People that initially didn't take our advice, are now coming back to us and telling us they wished they'd listened to us in the first place. More and more people are discovering that the information we gave them is indeed correct and in their best interest.

The financial jungle can be terrifying. People can get bad advice that hinders their retirement. In some cases, it can be an emotional battle.

One woman, let's call her Joan, came into my office in tears. Why? Her previous advisor told her she didn't have enough money! Naturally, she was devastated and no doubt in a panic. Who wouldn't be?

She couldn't retire. She didn't save enough. She was going to run out of money. Those are not words anyone wants to hear. Even though she had saved $600,000, she felt she had to go back to work. She was devastated. Her partner of twenty years came into our office with her. He asked me if there was something, anything we could do to help her.

It turns out the previous advisor was using a withdrawal rate that couldn't sustain the portfolio.

We decided to put some of her money in a one by five. You put the money in and don't touch it for a year. Then you can draw on it for five years.

Once that product is exhausted, we put her into another one that was a five by ten. As the first product dropped off, the other one picked up. She would have a continuous stream of income. At the end of the period, an annuity would kick in creating the lifetime income she needed of $3500 per month. She won't run out of money.

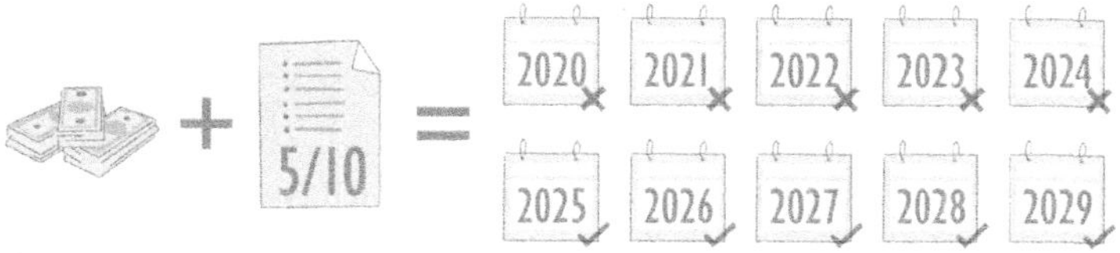

Initially, people may have qualms about running out of money. They worry that a set income per month will not have enough growth to beat back inflation. Nevertheless, we can prove to them that it is possible to stay ahead of inflation by having growth potential—a pay increase every year. Most of us don't see wage increases every single year we are in the work force. Yet, we can design a plan specifically for you that will give you that yearly raise and keep you ahead of inflation!

The best strategies you can use in guaranteeing your income streams is to maximize your Social Security to the fullest benefit. Then, supplement your income with an annuity and use the rest of your money for growth. It will keep you ahead of the curve and assure you that you're going to be okay!

> **!** A lot of fear mongering exists in the financial arena promulgated by the media.

Fear is a mighty leveler. Promoting fear is often used as a tool to sell products. Our retirement years can be very vulnerable and there are some people who take advantage of that.

We're even seeing advisors now that won't take on clients who have less than $500,000 saved! I don't believe in doing that! I don't have an exclusive club in my practice only open to certain investors with the right dollar amount. That's not how I operate. I'm willing to help anybody that comes to see me. It's just the way I am. Fully dedicated to helping people, I don't segregate them by their bank account. Yet, I know it's the trend now. People in all different circumstances are entitled to be helped. I'm there for them, even if others aren't.

Your money is important to you. It's important to me that we design a plan that fits your needs and takes care of your hard-earned money.

I'm also here to help with taxes and fees, reducing them or eliminating them entirely. By sitting down with my clients, I can advise them about withdrawing funds from their IRAs, 401ks, etc. It's my job to protect you and your interests. To do that, I study rules and regulations. My education is ongoing and will never stop. I will help you to learn those rules and regulations fortifying you in the knowledge you need to make the best decisions. Many people work with a minimum of three professionals (Financial advisor, tax professional, and attorney). So, I ask the question, how often do they talk?

Most of the time, the answer is never. Then how do you know you are getting the best possible growth, with the best possible tax advantages, and the best possible way to leave your legacy? The answer is: you don't, because they never talked. They could all be doing their jobs, but each needed to talk with the other to find out what was best for you! By working the S.I.M.P.L.E.™ plan, it is all coordinated together. Knowledge is power.

When you look at taxes, we must also consider tax efficiency. I had a man that came in to see me recently. I showed him how to draw out money before he reached the required minimum distribution age. His portfolio will be more efficient because taxes may go up in the future. By showing the client how to get his money out now, he's in a much better position to avoid taxes.

Many people today are saving, saving and saving and not drawing their money out. By not removing some of those funds, they risk higher taxes that may be on the horizon. We can show you how to withdraw your money at a lower tax rate and not get hit all at once when you withdraw your money in the future. This helps to determine guaranteed income.

Deferring certain withdrawals, and still adding to the account will mean the government has more to tax. We'll walk you through the steps and show you the best solution for you.

We sit down with clients and find out what their expenses are, what tax bracket they're in and design the best strategy for them and ensure the correct income stream. (We will cover taxes more in Chapter 7.)

You may be in a 22 percent tax bracket now. If you keep saving, and deferring, the tax rate down the road may be 40 percent. That's a significant jump. So, let's do something about that today!

Just remember, when determining your proper income stream, we will look at your lifestyle and your dreams. Together we can find the right approach to maximize your income, minimize your taxes, and help you live the retirement you've longed for.

Where is Market Risk in all of this? In the next chapter, we'll lay it all out for you!

CHAPTER 6

"M" IS FOR MARKET RISK

When someone comes to see me for financial advice, there are three key points we need to define. What are the client's goals? If we don't know the goals, we can't help guide the client. If we do not know the destination, how do we build the roadmap to get there? My clients consider me the GPS for their retirement.

The second area to define is: What strategies are we going to use to reach those goals? Without knowing all the goals and ranking their importance, it's difficult to find the correct strategy that will have positive results. A financial planner must know all the details possible to guide the client properly.

The third area to define: What tools are we going to use within those strategies? Obviously, some tools are better than others. The better the tool, the easier the work. That's true in all aspects of life. If you're on the golf course and your ball lands on the green, you're not going to use a driver to putt. You want to find the right club like the putter. A driver could work but it wouldn't be as effective.

Regarding financial planning, the tools I'm talking about that you would need in your tool bag are things like stocks, bonds, mutual funds, gold, annuities and real estate.

Often when people come into the office, they have seen other advisors who used different tools in the bag. For instance, the advisors may work for a company that has a vested interest in pushing certain tools that would be advantageous to their company but not necessarily to the client. Some advisors want to push certain pet stocks of theirs.

The company might have 500,000 shares of the stock. It may be a great company, but it may not be right for you.

> Not all the tools in the financial tool kit work for everyone.

It's much better to find the right tool for the individual client based on their needs and not rooted in something that would benefit the advisor's company. I am not captive to any certain company. As an independent advisor, I choose the tools for my clients based solely on their needs and not internal goals of a certain company. It simply wouldn't be fair to my client. Advisors that are not independent typically recommend tools from a limited toolbox.

Once I know my client's goals, then we discuss options that fit their needs.

Then I draw them a chart and list three things that clients look for.

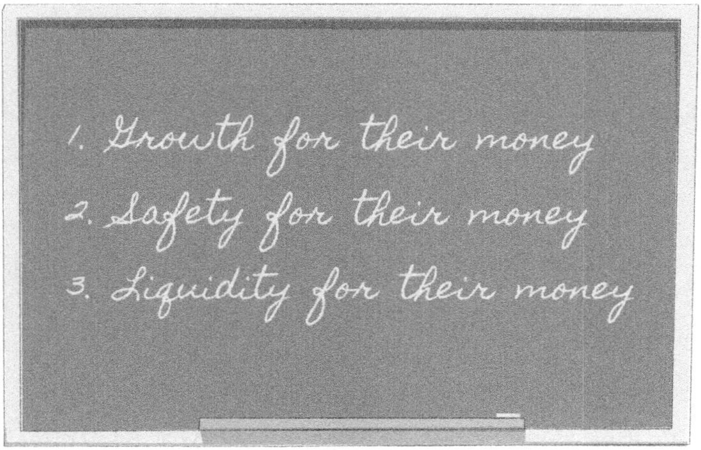

People want to be able to get their hands on their money when they need it. A certain portion of your money does need to be liquid so that you don't pay withdrawal penalties, and also if it needs to be used for emergencies.

Now, at this stage, I make sure that I tell my clients there is no magic bullet. There is no such thing as an investment that will give you growth, safety and liquidity. Naturally, there must be a trade-off. So, we look at choices that would best serve your needs and check off the most important boxes when meeting those needs.

SECURITIES

By the very definition of the word, Securities have the capacity for profit, but they also have the capacity for loss.

> Really, the term security is a play on words by Wall Street because there's nothing secure about it.

Let's look at securities and see what boxes they check.

Do they grow?	✓
Are they safe?	✗
Are securities liquid?	✓

Growth

Liquidity

Safety

Securities are liquid and you can call your broker and sell them. Overall, there is a risk to "Securities." It's up to the client to determine if they want to take that risk. Remember, guaranteed income is the key to real security. If you have enough guaranteed income, you may feel that being in the market is a risk you can afford to take.

PUTTING YOUR MONEY IN BANKS

Another area you can place your money is with banks with short-term instruments. You can get a savings or checking account, CDs and money markets. There is very limited opportunity for growth. However, there is safety because the funds are federally insured. Liquidity is there as well. You can go to your bank and cash out your accounts without a problem. While banks are secure, the limited growth is not the best place for the bulk of your funds. So, you get two out of three boxes checked. Unless you're going to put your money in a coffee can, there is one other option.

INSURANCE COMPANIES

Insurance companies offer life insurance, fixed annuities, and endowments. Can your funds grow? Absolutely! Are your funds safe in an insurance company?

Yes. Are your funds liquid enough to get your hands on the full cash value? No.

Most products offer a 10 percent penalty free withdrawal. This means you can get 10 percent of your money out, but it's not considered liquid in the eyes of the state.

As you can see, there is a trade-off with each of these tools. It's up to the individual client to assess what's important to them and to make their decisions based on their needs. If you go with securities, you give up safety. If you go with banks, you give up growth. If you go with insurance companies, you give up liquidity.

So, it all boils down to your goals and how to achieve them. The product doesn't matter. It's the result and the realization of your goals.

After all, it's your money, not mine.

That is the first thing I tell my clients. I'm not going to tell them they need to do this or that or invest here or there. That is up to the client after educating them about their options. I will, however, inform them of all the facts necessary to make an educated decision about what is right for them. We are a team.

Should a client tell me that he wants to spend all his money by age eighty and then live off the state after that, it is his decision. It's his money. Some people want to use their money while they're young enough to enjoy it! That's totally understandable. When you work hard all your life, it's up to you as to how you spend that hard-earned money.

Of course, some people have a much different response. Some people know they've got longevity in their family and don't want to spend all their money. They want to have enough funds to last them until they're ninety-five! It's not my position to make this decision. My job is to educate my clients and help them achieve their goals.

I have a confidentiality statement with my clients. I never reveal the full identity of my clients. Your goals, your money and how you handle them are sacrosanct.

To help you, I must fully understand your vision for your life. What do you want to do? What are your goals? Then we work together to achieve those goals. The client guides me on their needs and ambitions. I listen and take everything to heart. The client is in control and that's what I want.

It's critical for my clients to maintain control of their

retirement. This gives them freedom and peace of mind.

Obviously, at age thirty, your needs are different than they are at age sixty. A couple of downturns in the market won't impact your wealth as severely at thirty, but at sixty, that's another matter. Being knowledgeable about your money is important at every stage.

You must understand distribution and the Sequence of Returns. Sequence of Returns evaluates the order of the returns on your money. You may end up with a lower rate of return on your money than you originally expected. Therefore, it's my job to inform my clients so they can make the best decisions for their families.

You may decide to put some of your money into great mutual funds that are averaging 15 percent returns, but you may not realize that those moderate investments may lose 30 percent if the markets suffer a downturn. It's happened before and it's pivotal to look at the history.

I explain the trade-offs to people and make sure they fully understand the ins and outs, so they are not caught unaware. Once we determine the best vehicle for my clients that check off the right boxes, my clients know they're moving their money where it's supposed to be.

Maybe you're willing to give up some liquidity for safety or you may prefer growth over safety. I'll point out all the pros and cons and make sure that all the risks are explained so you can feel secure in your decisions. I do a yearly or even quarterly review with my clients to ensure that their needs are being met and that their investments are performing the way they should.

Things change every year in this industry and I'm always studying the changes and their ramifications. I don't want to overlook something that would cause problems for my clients. We follow specific steps to ensure the client's money is working for them and not someone else.

Every one of the steps is in the S.I.M.P.L.E.™ Plan. Further, I believe in total transparency. I do not want to put my clients in any situation where there is a conflict of interest. My first concern is your bottom line. That's the way it should be, and I won't have it any other way.

With the stock market, we hear a lot of hype that if you want growth, you need to be in the markets. That's not entirely true. We also hear about paper losses and that the market will bounce back.

If you lose money, it's gone! Sure, you'll hear that the market will be ok. It'll bounce back. "It always does!" Well, those losses aren't just on paper. They're real. The funny thing is you don't hear advisors talking about paper gains. Or that the gains are not real. This should make us pause and rethink our positions.

Brokers cannot advise on all aspects of financial investments. They can only address securities. My licenses allow me to advise on both the market and other financial vehicles. Why not marry the market and your other investments to get the best of both worlds? That's what I recommend, if my clients want to have some money in the market for growth but are also looking for safety. Financial decisions aren't a one or the other type of choice. It's looking at the bigger picture and coloring that picture with my client's needs and goals.

MARKET VOLATILITY

After the crash of 2008 and the most recent crash in 2020, people worried about market volatility. It's something that looms on the horizon and it's prudent to be cautious. We can see by the Dow that the markets are up, and some say they're artificially inflated.

I look at market volatility like this:

If you pump up a balloon, it expands. You keep pumping more air in the balloon and eventually the balloon will burst. The same is true with the market. Past history shows that the market is volatile and will go up and down.

> Quantitative easing is when a central bank decides to purchase a set amount of assets and government bonds to instill liquidity into the economy.

We're hearing about another round of quantitative easing. We've also had bailouts and holding interest rates down just to keep the economy on its feet. What is the result? We have an artificially manufactured economy! It's done to keep the economy relevant.

We should let the economy play out and adjust itself. We might experience a 20 percent or 30 percent drop, but it would be back to where it's supposed to be—naturally. Once again, if we look at history, the market will bounce back over time. But remember these loses can be more devastating to your retirement due to your time horizon.

Wall Street has its checks and balances to keep things in line.[11] Prior to 1929, the markets didn't have anything in place. Consequently, the markets tanked in October of that year sending the economy and a large section of the population into a tailspin.

When powerful and wealthy people make decisions and waves in the market, other people tend to follow them. It's a mob mentality.[12] That mentality may cause a ripple effect for bad or for worse. When we finally see that it may be the right time to buy stocks, it may be too late. All the good stuff is gone. Ray Dalio mentioned this. Dalio is a billionaire investor and hedge fund manager who founded Bridgewater Associates, the world's largest hedge fund.

Think about this: With the S&P, the Dow and NASDAQ at all-time highs, how many of us hear from our brokers that the markets are doing well? You're making

---

11 https://www.thebalance.com/black-thursday-1929-what-happened-and-what-caused-it-3305817
Or
https://www.federalreservehistory.org/essays/banking_panics_1930_31

12 https://www.cnbc.com/2018/10/17/ray-dalio-this-is-the-biggest-mistake-that-most-investors-make.html
And/or
https://www.cnbc.com/2018/09/14/bridgewater-associates-ray-dalio-on-anniversary-of-financial-crisis.html

a ton of money, but it's time to pull out? No one says that.

In 2020, when the crash hit, what were people told? Hold on! The market will come back!

> It seems to me that Wall Street is like a casino. They don't care if you win or lose.

The more you play in the stock market, the more they make. It is the matter of keeping you in the game. That's a disconcerting thought.

Now there's the Rule of 100 that comes into play, as I mentioned before. It's a theory that some people espouse. The Rule of 100 helps to define the percentage of your assets that should be at risk vs. safety. For example, I'm fifty-two; that means I should hold 48 percent of my money in risk investments. Yes, I do have stocks, but I also have life insurance and annuities. I'm also still working and making an income. Following the Rule of 100 is an easy guideline to define these percentages and take into account your time horizon. I can't possibly recommend something to my clients that I don't practice. It wouldn't be right. I follow the S.I.M.P.L.E.™ Plan because it works, and it will work for you!

If you're seventy-five and want to get into the market, the outlook is much different. While I'm still working, I can afford to lose some money and have stop/losses in place. At seventy-five, it wouldn't be wise to gamble with your money. There is a time and a place for everything.

Some clients have come into my office and told me they were in a moderate fund and they had nothing to worry about. They didn't realize they could lose 30 percent! I asked one guy if he had $1 million, and he lost $300,000, would he be upset? The guy said of course he would. He just didn't realize that his funds were exposed to that much risk. Then I asked him if he would like to do something about it. Absolutely!

I'm not okay with losing 30 percent nor should you be! Who tells people to enter investments like that in retirement? Once I educate my clients about the possible exposure to this amount of risk, they tend to look toward safer investments.

We must realize that every person's definition of "safe" is not the same. That's true with the investment world. They might agree about the Rule of 100, but when it comes to safety that's another matter. It's completely subjective and one risk size doesn't fit all.

IS THERE A RISK ASSOCIATED WITH BONDS?

There is a risk with bonds and their interest rates. Bonds are interest rate sensitive. Interest rates are low today. If you're using bonds as a safety net, look at this analogy that I relate to my clients: When you were a kid and played on the teeter totter with your buddy, if you were down, where was your buddy? People will say the buddy is up. And when you're up, where is your buddy? He's down. Now you understand the relationship between bonds and interest rates. If you're using bonds as a safety net, you may want to rethink that position.

I had a client come into my office not long ago. He's an engineer and used to analytical thinking. He told me his 401k over the past fifteen years earned 20 percent. I didn't argue with him but instead, I asked him to bring in his statements and we'd go over them. He told me there was no reason to do that. That his financial advisor at that time went over them with him and confirmed he made 20 percent.

I asked him to appease me and bring the statements in anyway. It's similar to a doctor/patient relationship, a patient needs to supply all the information they can for the doctor to make an accurate diagnosis. The same is true for my clients.

Well, he brought the statements in. What my client forgot was that he was still contributing 10 percent of his income into the 401k while his employer was putting in 6 percent. So, he's only making about 3 percent on his money because he was still actively making deposits with his own money. He was exposed to fancy and confusing math. If an engineer can be misled, anyone can be.

I went back over the statements, fifteen years-worth to prove the point. This happens all the time. People come and tell me how well their company plans are doing, when that's not necessarily the case. The worst part is, they don't realize it. They may realize it down the road but then it will be too late. Those statements show an average rate of return. They do not show the actual rate of return. That's important to remember!

Frequently, people have a misplaced loyalty for their investment advisors, and they don't want to leave them. Change can be difficult. In the case of your money, a second opinion or a new voice can shed light on your true financial picture.

Wall Street is no different from stores. They buy inventory. Sometimes they can sell off that inventory with no problem. Still, there are other times when certain products don't sell well and the store, or in this case, Wall Street, gets stuck with a lot of bad inventory. What do they do? They sell it off.

They push it until they diminish the inventory. Is it right for you? Probably not. Is it right they push that inventory on unsuspecting clients? No!

Goldman Sachs did that. They sent out emails to all their people and told them that a particular investment was lousy and to get rid of it.[13] What did their employees do? They got rid of it and a whole lot of people got stuck with a terrible stock! As for Goldman Sachs? They made $300 million. They knew it was junk. They sold it anyway!

With the market, it's best to do your homework and ask a reputable financial advisor about what is right for you. I'm here to help and to advise you. I'm here for you.

Next up we'll cover Personal Taxes!!

13 https://slate.com/news-and-politics/2010/04/the-senate-tries-to-get-goldman-sachs-to-admit-it-sold-america-a-pile-of-crap.html

CHAPTER 7

"P" IS FOR PERSONAL TAXES

When I was sixteen, my dad gave me a 1965 Ford Mustang! Talk about being happy! Okay, it was a fixer-upper and it needed lots of repairs. Still, I thought it was worth it. We didn't have many extras when I was growing up. So, this car was very special to me. I had to buy gas for it and pay for insurance—not an easy deal for a kid of sixteen. If I wanted to hang out with my friends, to go to football games and to tailgate, I had to take care of the expenses.

Paying for everything meant I had to get a job. I worked for a major grocery store at the time. They paid me $3 per hour, minimum wage back then. I got the job during the summer and was able to work forty hours per week. My paycheck was expected to be $120 at the end of the week. I was in for a surprise.

On Friday, I went to the payroll lady for my check. I couldn't wait. I had things to do and places to go in my Mustang. I got my check and looked at it. It wasn't $120! Instead, I saw some interesting items on the deductions.

"Who's this FICA character?" I asked the payroll lady.

Then I said, "What's this about Social Security? What is that?"

The payroll lady laughed, and I didn't understand why. I scratched my head the whole way home. It was horrible. I counted on that $120 but got less. I decided I had better go and talk to my grandpa about it. I showed him the paystub and asked him about the deductions.

"Oh, that's Uncle Sam," he said.

Uncle Sam? I couldn't believe it!

> Immediately, I learned that if you're going to make money in this life, it's going to be taxed.

Taxes are okay, but none of us wants to pay more than our fair share. I still felt off center about the whole thing. Afterall, my bubble burst.

"What can we do about it, Grandpa?"

"I think we'll go buy you something. It'll make you feel better!"

Great financial advice, Grandpa! It wasn't exactly what I wanted to hear. I got out the newspaper, we didn't have the internet then and I found a Pioneer radio and cassette deck for sale. Circuit City was selling it as the latest technology. Gone were the old 8-Track players. I thought I had to have it. It would really be great to have it installed in the Mustang! I'd be set.

I grabbed the radio and headed to the checkout. To my surprise, it didn't ring up $99.95. The price was more because there was sales tax! Chalk up another lesson. If you're going to spend money, it's going to be taxed.

Interest rate, CD, and 1099

For the next year, I saved every penny I made. Eventually, I went to Liberty Bank and bought a CD. Then the interest rate was 15 percent. Heck of a deal!

I knew my money would increase and not decrease. Well, at the end of the year, I got a 1099 and you guessed it. I was taxed on the money the CD made. Saving money and getting interest means you're going to pay taxes.

It was baffling to me and infuriating. Not long after that, my grandpa died. We had an estate auction. I didn't know that if you die, your estate gets taxed. Each time I turned around, it seemed like I was being taxed. We all are.

> The moral of the story is that we're never going to beat Uncle Sam. It's impossible.

Therefore, it's our job to be as tax efficient as possible. That means we need to learn all the options we have and use them to our advantage.

In my seminars, I normally use this analogy: The Bible has some 800,000 words. The IRS Tax Code has 3.8 million words or more. Few of us have the time to read through all the code, but that doesn't mean we should excuse ourselves from what is in the code.

We need to seek the advice of a well-versed financial advisor. I stay on top of all the changes that are going on and help my clients to avoid paying too much in taxes.

It's not what you make, but what you get to keep in retirement!

Being aware of your tax threshold is important. You need to know what you can deduct and what you can't. You need to know what you can contribute and what you can't contribute. We are supposed to pay taxes, but we don't want to overpay. It's in our best interest to pay what we rightfully owe and not a penny more.

TAX EFFICIENT OPTIONS

Looking at tax efficiency for my clients, it really comes down to the individual's needs and goals. Tax deferred accounts work well. Other options include IRAs and Roth IRAs. There are many ways that we can create tax efficiency. If you're looking at lowering your taxes now, you can use IRAs or SEP IRAs, where that money is deducted off your gross income lowering your tax bracket now. That's an immediate benefit.

A SEP IRA is an IRA that allows business owners to offer a retirement plan for their employees when it may not be possible by other means. The IRS has some guidelines for the SEP IRAs.

The SEP IRAs allow employees to stockpile money. An employee can also combine an IRA with the SEP IRA, which are easy to set up. Contributions are tax deductible.

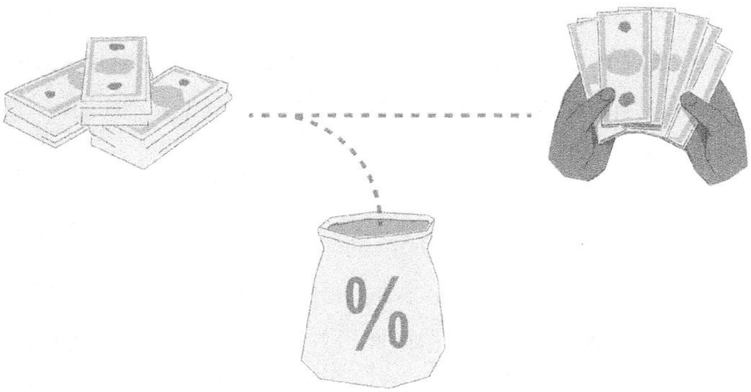

We don't know where taxes are going to go. Most likely they are as low as they will go. The likelihood exists for taxes to go up. It's best to have a plan of action to stay ahead of the tax curve. Anticipating that taxes will increase, it's a good idea to convert some of your 401k and IRA money into a Roth.

The reason I recommend conversion is that if you do that then after five years, the principal and interest are tax free for the rest of your life!

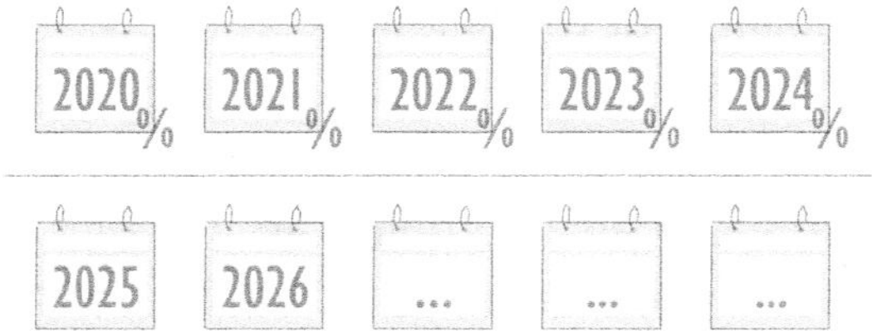

An inevitable rise in taxes won't matter because you're taken care of. I've already done that with some of my money. It's a reassuring thought to know that the money will be tax free.

For people who are worried about taxes rising, it can create the need to hoard money and to scrimp and save any way possible. The concern is that with all that money stored up, there's that much more money to be taxed by the government. The tax rate will probably be higher, and you will, of course, pay much more. That's counterproductive and isn't tax efficient.

CASE IN POINT

One couple I know came to me for help. They owned a septic tank business and a chicken coop business. A situation arose when the husband died, and his wife, Dot, was left not knowing what to do. Her financial advisor at the time told her not to pull the money out of her accounts because she was going to be taxed on it. What he didn't tell her was that it would be her last year to file married filing jointly. The following year Dot would have to file as single.

The best thing she could have done was to pull as much money out from her accounts that she would be comfortable with while she could still file married filing jointly because her tax rates would have been lower. Her previous advisor missed that critical point.

> Some advisors when they have Assets Under Management, don't want their clients to withdraw any funds because it greatly hits the advisor's bottom line.

It's unfortunate because the client suffers. I told Dot my advice and said that she didn't have to take my word for it. I encouraged her to call her CPA and to verify what I said. The CPA confirmed what I had told her. I'm glad she got a second opinion. I'm all for it. My client's best interests are what matter.

LIFE INSURANCE

Another great way to avoid taxes is life insurance.[14] The death benefits are not taxable with a properly named beneficiary. However, estate taxes are a different subject. Estate taxes are not federally taxed if the money is under $11.5 million. If it is over that amount, then the funds are taxed at a rate of 40 percent. If you have a trust it doubles and goes to $23 million.

What many people don't understand is that we're not talking about estate tax exemptions. We are talking about IRA and 401k money, what we call pretax dollars, that would be inherited and have an earned income tax. Your heirs would have to take a lump sum distribution or draw that money out over a period of ten years.

> Combining 401ks and IRAs is a good thing and people are not penalized.

It's a good deal for people who haven't been able to save enough. I'm not a fan of lifting the RMD or Re-

14 https://www.irs.gov/faqs/interest-dividends-other-types-of-income/life-insurance-disability-insurance-proceeds

quired Minimum Distribution age to 72 instead of 70 1/2. While it does allow you to put money away longer, I think the government knows they are going to raise taxes. That will hurt you in the long run. Deferring your distribution will mean that you have more money to tax. It's good for the government but not good for you.

The problem I see right now and especially lately, is that people just don't know what's going on when it comes to taxes and retirement. Just recently, I had eight to ten people in my office in one week discussing this very thing. It's like a well-kept secret that I believe should be shared. I do share with my clients. I printed out the 2020 tax summary for them to help them understand what they needed to know. I invited them to take the summary home and to read it thoroughly so they can make intelligent and informed decisions about their money and their future.

If you go to an advisor who only understands the securities side of things and doesn't know about taxes and Social Security, you won't get the complete picture. The advisor may tell you you'll make 8 percent, but you'll net 5 percent. It's imperative to find an advisor who knows taxes, insurance and annuities and securities to best advise you on the overall picture. Being well-versed across the board, a competent advisor can guide you and help you to protect your hard-earned money from taxes.

HEALTH SAVINGS ACCOUNTS

Health Savings Accounts or HSAs can help you avoid taxes. Having money put aside for healthcare is important. Medicare and even supplemental insurance might not be enough, given the cost of medical care today. By putting money into your HSA, it rolls over year after year and you don't need to worry about it. When it comes to withdrawal, it's like an IRA. It will come directly off your income.

STARTING A BUSINESS TO HELP WITH TAXES

Starting a business isn't for everyone. It can be demanding. Retirement years aren't meant to be stressful. Should you decide on buying rental property, it's good for taxes but you also have the upkeep and the problems that may arise with renters and the property itself.

Owning rental property puts you on-call for your tenants and those calls could come in the middle of the night. Swapping out a refrigerator or having a leak fixed aren't necessarily major issues. Yet, roofs, furnaces and air conditioners need to be replaced. It could be expensive and add to your stress. Some people have the stamina to do this or to run other businesses. If you're one of those people who enjoys running your own business, it may be a great strategy for you when keeping taxes under control. Choosing to run a business in retirement takes thought and self-reflection. If it works for you, great!

LONG-TERM CAPITAL GAINS

Long-term capital gains are taxed at a lower rate than short-term gains. The capital gains issue isn't really a fair one. If you get capital gains, when does the government want the tax money? Within the year the gains were realized. But if you have a capital loss, can you write all that off the first year? No! If you make money, the government wants it right away. If you lose money, you're only allowed to write off $3000 per year on that loss. It's not fair!

MUNICIPAL BONDS AND TAXES

We touched on municipal bonds in another chapter. Yes, if you take a state bond, they aren't federally taxed. Nevertheless, the interest you make counts against your Social Security. So, you are being taxed.

ANNUITIES

Annuities will help you now because taxes are deferred, but upon your death, your heirs will receive the benefit. If the taxes haven't been paid, guess who will be stuck with the tax bill? Your heirs.

Deciding what you want to do to keep taxes in line is important. When I was sixteen and just learning the ropes regarding income and taxes, I had no idea about the ramifications of everything. Many people today find themselves much like I was at sixteen. Although they do understand Uncle Sam and payroll deductions, sales tax and other taxes, they are still in the dark about the taxes that will hit their lives during their retirement years.

Finding the right advisor to help you through the maze of the tax code and to help you construct a solid foundation for your future depends on the skills of the advisor. They are not created equal. When it comes to retirement planning, it's crucial to find the advisor who can work with you across the board from securities to Social Security, annuities and IRAs. Just like no two clients are alike in their financial planning, no two advisors are alike.

I make sure that my clients are educated and confident about their financial future. I work for you, not some big company with an agenda all its own. I'm here to help you keep the money you earned and to help you with your taxes.

In the next chapter, we're going to look at Long-Term Care. How can you prepare for the possibilities? Let's find out!

CHAPTER 8

"L" IS FOR LONG-TERM CARE

Long-term care is something none of us really wants to think about or even talk about. When I first started in this business, I started in long-term care. That's all I did for four years. I learned quite a lot. The whole concept of long-term care for me is a personal one.

As I mentioned before, had my grandmother agreed to go to a nursing home, my mother's Alzheimer's might not have been triggered. She was under incredible stress taking care of my grandmother. I don't want other people to go through what my mother went through because of the lack of long-term care coverage. Long-term care is something that affects everyone in the family, one way or another.

When we're younger, we don't really think or worry about long-term care, but we should. Time has a way of gaining on us and before you know it, the need for care is suddenly upon us. Whether it's a parent, spouse or some other family member, the likelihood of having to enter the long-term care realm is high. Again, longevity does have its downside. However, if we prepare for the possibilities, we know the funds will be there for us.

Over the years, several long-term care stories stick out in my mind. One recent story is a good example of what families face when it comes to long-term care.

A sixty-three-year-old woman, let's call her Sally, came into my office and told me that she had $100,000 that wasn't really doing anything. She was married to a man who was seventy-five. After some fact-finding about her goals, and after our discussion, Sally decided to put her money into a long-term care generating contract, giving her $350.000 in benefits. This was coverage for her only. Unfortunately, her husband did not qualify due to health conditions—long term care does not take your money into account, only your age and your health.

That was five years ago. She recently returned to the office with her stepdaughter. An issue had arisen with her husband. He suffers from Parkinson's and after some falls, his memory was further impaired. They could no longer take care of him at home. His safety and care were in jeopardy.

It became necessary to put the man into a memory care clinic. The cost of the care is $6,000 per month. However, the cost is just for room and board. Anything beyond that falls on the family to cover. If there are field trips to the movies or other things, the facility doesn't cover them.

The situation was bad. Her husband's care costs needed to be covered but I pointed out to Sally that she had needs, too. She couldn't stop living because of the circumstances. It's a quandary we all face in our lives when a family member needs long-term care.

This woman had gotten some bad advice from previous advisors who didn't go into much detail when it came to the spin-down costs.

> The lack of credible information is certainly problematic especially when people are faced with the big decisions, and the high costs surrounding long-term care.

The Washington Post put out an article that discusses the long-term care crisis in America:

https://www.washingtonpost.com/business/2019/10/31/many-families-long-term-care-costs-are-horrifying/

The high costs of long-term care not only encompass the patient, but many times, the high cost hits the unpaid caregiver who must quit a job to care for their family member. It's only natural that this woman had concerns about how to cover the long-term care for her husband. When she didn't get all her questions answered, it fostered new questions.

Sally didn't know if she could get out of some contracts or not. She went to the nursing home with her questions, but to be honest, they really didn't have a grasp on the situation. The woman and her stepdaughter were left in the lurch.

We discussed the needs and areas that had to be addressed and we got them straightened out and put on a clear path forward. This woman was a professor at a prestigious university and consequently had a good pension, which could take care of the long-term care bill for her husband. The problem was there was no protection from inflation.

We looked at growing income from annuities that would also help. A very critical problem would arise should she die before her husband. That would leave a huge gap that must be filled to cover her husband's needs, since he could no longer benefit from her pension.

Originally, she was single when she opted into her pension with the university, so her husband was not included as a beneficiary. Many people are facing similar circumstances. It's important to know just what you have and how it will be disbursed to spouses should you die.

Without her husband's ability to draw on that pension, their current assets would have to go through a drawdown to pay his long-term care. Should he live for over five more years, and should his wife precede him in death, his daughters would have serious financial gaps.

> Long-term care coverage is essential to preserve your assets!

As far as I know and from what my experience has shown, there are only three ways to provide for long-term care:

1. You self-insure against long-term care costs by using your checkbook.

2. You go with an insurance company and use their checkbook.

3. You draw down all your assets to nothing and then go on Medicaid.

Rules vary from state to state on the spin down process. It's a good idea to know all you can about those rules. Here's where the family's lifestyle comes into play.

With insurance, the spouse in the long-term care facility will have coverage and if there's a surviving spouse at home, they may need to change their lifestyle a bit, but they will not become impoverished.

Should the Medicaid route need to be employed, the spouse at home may not be able to continue the current lifestyle due to the mandated spin down process.

I saw a study recently that claimed that one out of two married couples over the age of sixty-five will need long-term care.[15] That puts things into a whole new light. The odds are not in your favor.

15 https://www.morningstar.com/articles/957487/must-know-statistics-about-long-term-care-2019-edition

When I do my dinner seminars and it comes time to talk about long-term care, I start off the talk with a little joke. I ask them this question:

Who here is going to a nursing home?

I know I'm not. Not one person raises their hand. That's funny, in a way. Just look at the odds.

Then I say that's really something. Not one of us in this room is going to a nursing home. I go on to tell them we should feel badly for the people not in the seminar because we just increased their chances of going into long-term care.

The audience finally gets it. At first, we can laugh it off, but statistics speak for themselves. One out of every two married couples will need long-term care.

Okay, so we need to do something about it.

I've found out that people really don't get the Medicaid process. I use an analogy that works. I ask the people at the seminar if they've seen the movie *Titanic*. People all nod their heads and say, "Yeah!"

Then I ask them about the scene at the end of the movie where people are floating in the water. "Yeah! Yeah," they answer back.

Well, Medicaid is like those people in the water. They're out there floating, darn near freezing to death and about to drown. That's Medicaid, which will throw you a life preserver at the last moment. Do any of us want to go there?

Remember, we may have a spouse who won't need long-term care even if we do. Do we want our loved ones in that situation? Why put yourselves or your spouse in that predicament of losing everything before the life preserver is tossed to you?

Getting long-term care is dependent upon two things. First, it's dependent on age. Second, it's dependent on health.

1. Age
2. Health

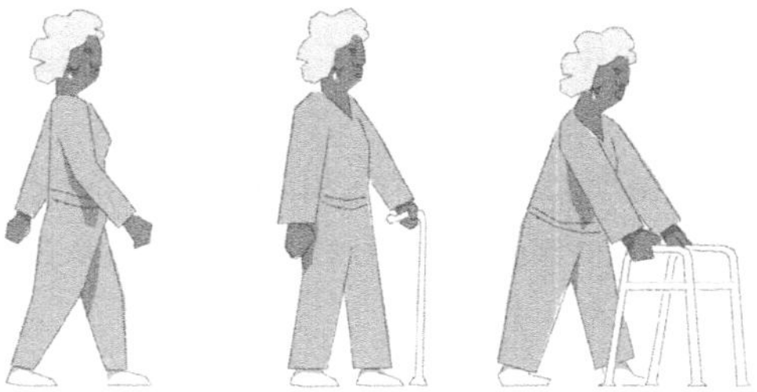

I let everyone know upfront that the insurance company doesn't care about your money. Let's face it. If you knew that you would need the coverage, you'd pay anything to get it! If the insurance company knows you're going to need it, they won't approve you! They couldn't possibly take in enough premiums before you need it to make it a risk worth taking for them.

> Long-term care coverage is based on the unknown.

MORBIDITY VS. MORTALITY

Insurance companies use what is called a morbidity table. To be clear, there are two tables. One is the mortality table and one is the morbidity table. A distinct difference exists between the two.

Mortality applies to life insurance. Morbidity applies to health insurance.

So, what's the risk of a person aged seventy-five with Type 2 diabetes, medication controlled, not insulin dependent that hasn't had an overnight stay in the hospital for five years?

What is this person's risk of needing long-term care? That's what insurance companies look for. Premium structures are based on health and the odds you'll need long-term care. If you have a heart problem, you'll probably get long-term care coverage because your risks of dying are greater and that reduces the insurance company's payout to long-term care.

Let's flip the coin!

If you have disabling arthritis, you will probably get life insurance, but you will not get long-term care. The arthritis will not kill you, but you will be more prone to falls and falls may lead to long-term care.

The odds are stacked against you. Yet, I've always said, it's better to have it and not need it, than to need it and not have it! I'm totally upfront with my clients. If you have the money for long-term care, then get it. If you don't have the money, don't get it.

At seminars, I get questions that follow that statement. Why should I pay for something I won't need?

My answer is in the form of a question.

How many of you own a house?

Hands will go up all over the room. I tell them I own my house, too. Next, I ask them if anyone in the room hopes their house is on fire?

"What?" they ask in unison.

Why do you have homeowner's insurance if you aren't sitting here hoping your house is on fire?

The crowd will answer that they have the insurance in case they need it. It's the same thing with long-term care.

It's been said that long-term care coverage is for the rich. Sure, they can afford it. The average person may not be able to. Still, we're not dealing with just the one person who may need it but the spouse who will suffer the aftershock of the spin down to get to Medicaid and the life preserver. Long-term care coverage may not be important to you, but it is important to your spouse.

I used the example of the costs per month for the memory care facility being $6,000 per month. Yet, that's not for a full-blown nursing home, where costs are normally running $9,000 per month depending on where you are in the country. In the northeast, costs are much higher. Can you afford $9,000 per month for long-term care?

It's best to get into long-term care coverage between the ages of fifty and sixty. Once you're over sixty-five, premium costs are much higher. The problem with younger people is that they feel they're invincible and don't need the coverage. They think they'll live forever. Most of the younger generation lives in the moment.

When you get older, you realize the possibilities loom and you become more aware of your chances for long-term care.

It's essential to have a plan. I work with my clients to develop the best plan possible for them and their families. No one wants their families to become destitute. No one wants to see their hard-earned money dwindle or spin down to nothing. I make sure that every client is asked about long-term care.

Sharing the importance of the S.I.M.P.L.E. ™ Plan shows the direct correlation of the plan's individual strategies. The plan is much stronger when all the strategies are employed. Together, we will find the best path for you and protect your money.

Do you want to spend $300 or $400 per day in long-term care or do you just want the basics covered? We can figure it out together. The average stay in long-term care is about two to two-and one-half years.

In the next chapter, we'll look at Estate Planning and how you can leave a legacy for your family!

CHAPTER 9

"E" IS FOR ESTATE PLANNING: LEAVING A LEGACY FOR YOUR LOVED ONES

I've said many times, we aren't promised tomorrow. We only have today. Unfortunately, the loss of a loved one is an universal truth. When we lose someone we love, someone close to us, it drives home the fact that we are only here for a short time. I learned this hard lesson eighteen years ago, when my cousin Frankie was in a horrific accident. His accident hit me hard and changed how I view life forever.

James Franklin "Frankie" Higdon and I weren't just cousins. We were really like brothers. He was a wonderful guy, highly regarded and loved. Frankie worked for an elevator company and lived about an hour and a half away in the country.

The day before Easter, Frankie came to town to visit with some friends. He didn't want to spend the night because the family had small children and he didn't want to interfere with their Easter celebrations.

That Saturday night it was raining, and Frankie was driving the company truck home. The truck was also carrying a load of propane. Well, Frankie went around a bend and because of the wet road, the truck hydroplaned. He ended up hitting a telephone poll. Sadly, the propane ignited almost instantly. Frankie was engulfed with flames and he ran down the road trying to get help. A farmer saw what happened and immediately called 911.

A helicopter airlifted him to the University of Louisville Hospital Burn Center. Unbelievably, Frankie lived for twelve days. There wasn't enough morphine in the world to ease his pain. His family and mine were devastated. To see someone you love suffer excruciating pain with little hope of relief was so awful, words can't describe the anguish.

We prayed day and night for the Lord to either heal him or just to take him home. Those memories are etched in my mind and will never be erased. The doctors and nurses at the hospital, who deal with burn cases all the time, said they had never seen burns that bad in their entire careers! I can't imagine the agony Frankie was going through. Often, we don't understand the rhyme nor the reason for things. Only God knows.

The images of Frankie lying in that bed will never go away. He was covered in bandages and his head was three times its normal size because of the fluid build-up. On the twelfth day, the Good Lord called Frankie home! It was a blessing. While we would miss him terribly, we knew his suffering was over.

Frankie was only two years younger than I. He was at an age when planning for your untimely death was not even a thought. When we grew up, Frankie lived next door to us for years. His family eventually moved to the other side of town. We no longer went to the same school, but we did see each other often. Frankie and I ended up going to the same colleges and we became even closer.

Frankie had two young daughters, Ashley and Hannah, and they're wonderful girls. I'm sure Frankie is very proud of them. After his death, his wife Sherry moved with them back to South Dakota where she grew up. Ashley now has a boy and a girl, and I think about Frankie and what an awesome grandpa he would have been.

Hannah, who was partially deaf, never let her challenges deter her. She was crowned the South Dakota Snow Queen and has gone on to create an amazing life for herself.

The lessons I learned through all of that have lingered and made me appreciate living in the moment, doing all I can for everyone I meet. It is never too early to plan, especially when there are children involved. I don't want to miss an opportunity to help someone. Being a financial advisor has put me in a unique position to make sure that my clients have the best possible advice about their money.

I can't stress enough how important Estate Planning is and how crucial it is for both spouses to be actively involved in the process.

So, let's look at the various aspects of Estate Planning to give you a better foundation to build your legacy.

> The Secure Act that was signed January 1, 2020 impacted estates. Now, under the Secure Act, the non-spouse beneficiary must take out the funds over a minimum of ten years.

The stretch IRA was taken out of the estate picture. A stretch IRA was an IRA that could be inherited by non-spouses and could be passed down through the generations where the IRA would have the advantage of tax-free funds that could grow in it. That change altered the estate landscape.

Now, under the Secure Act, the non-spouse beneficiary must take out the funds over a minimum of ten years.

The government gets its taxes up front. The stretch IRA meant you didn't have to use a GST or Generational Skipping Trust. Taxes are likely to go up, so deferring the taxes on the inheritance wouldn't be a good thing. It proves the old maxim that every coin has two sides.

The good news is that you can still contribute to an IRA after age seventy and a half and up to age seventy-two. It's now possible for people to create their own pensions without their 401ks.

If you'll recall about the husband who was to go to a Memory Care clinic, well, he died shortly after. I visited with his family who wanted to do a Roth IRA after his death. I told them that was no longer possible. That leaves the family with a big decision to make.

How is their father's money going to be disbursed?

I spoke to them about their options and we went over the tax situation and whether they should move that money into an IRA.

We discussed things for two hours and helped them with the claim's forms and the death certificate. The family decided they wanted me to be their financial advisor. So, I applied for my Texas insurance and securities licenses.

His wife decided to take a bunch of money out of their IRA, but not enough to place her into a higher tax bracket. I am glad we had that chat *before* her husband died. We were able to put these plans into place prior to his death so she could have peace of mind during the grieving process.

> It's so important for spouses to work together planning their estate.

It's a well-known fact that women normally outlive

their husbands. According to the World Health Organization, or WHO, women worldwide live an average of six to eight years longer than men.

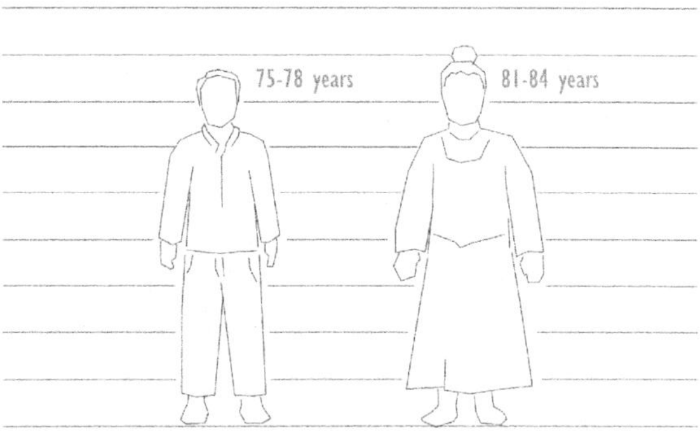

https://www.who.int/gho/women_and_health/mortality/situation_trends_life_expectancy/en/.

Since women do live longer than men, they must really be involved in all the financial aspects of life. Making important decisions following the death of a loved one isn't recommended. The time to make the decisions is before a person dies.

It isn't always the spouse but the entire family that is affected. Having things sewn up before a death occurs is preferable.

The wife in the above-mentioned case was able to make important decisions. We looked at her current income and she decided she had more than enough income upon which to live. I asked her what she wanted to do with the extra money.

She thought about it and concluded that she could spend it or leave it to her stepfamily. Never having been married before and with no other children, it seemed like a great option.

She wanted to make sure her family wouldn't need to pay taxes and that they wouldn't have to work things out in court. We looked at the situation. She had three beneficiaries. I told her she could afford to leave each one $500,000. All she needed to do was buy a $1.5 million life insurance policy and her family would get their inheritance tax free and they could avoid probate.

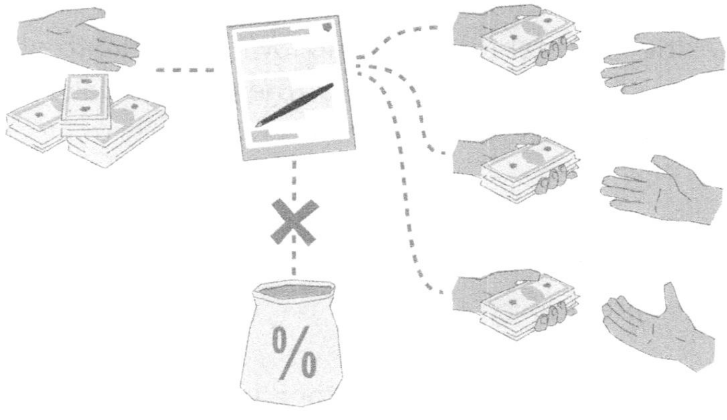

As for her, she could live worry free for the rest of her life knowing that she had enough money to live on and that her beneficiaries would be well-cared for.

KISS ME WILL OR FINAL LOVE LETTER

When a spouse passes, the surviving spouse can inherit the money without the worry of taxes and probate! What a final gift we can make to our spouses! Just knowing that is reassuring. However, the eventual death of the surviving spouse changes things and money left to beneficiaries may be taxed. It's like you get one death free and the other is not.

With a large percentage of my clients, the role of estate and financial planning usually falls to just one of the spouses. This one spouse takes care of estate planning and if they die before the other, the surviving spouse is at a disadvantage, especially if they have not been part of the process. The spouse responsible for the estate and financial planning is usually the one who also writes the checks for bills and essentials. They know all about their financial situation. The non-financial spouse is often kept in the dark. By bringing both parties into the planning stage, neither are left in the dark when it comes to the distribution of the estate.

By alleviating worry and concerns, the transition following a death will be much easier. The surviving spouse will be secure financially and the beneficiaries may be taken care of after the surviving spouse dies.

> **!** Putting off critical decisions about estate planning puts your wealth at risk and leaves room for anxiety and stress.

Let's break it down. All estate planning is answering the question: How much more money can I put in my pocket now? That's the basics and I'm here to help you put as much money into your pocket and not have it taxed.

If you go through probate, the estate is locked down for at least six months or even longer. For instance, the average time in Kentucky is about a year and one half. That's a long time. Further, creditors will have a shot at the estate. Children will not be able to access the money until the judge signs an order that the estate is cleared. It can be a waiting game. Bypassing probate is the sensible thing to do and will save money.

CHOOSING BETWEEN A TRUST OR A WILL

In my opinion, if you own a house, you should have a trust, rather than a will. A trust can help:

1. Keep your assets out of probate.
2. Creditors will be kept away from your assets.
3. Assets designated for minors can be handled without probate.
4. Disabled beneficiaries can have protection of government funds.
5. Minimize estate taxes.

With a trust, if you die on Friday at noon, at 12:01 PM, whoever you named as executor can distribute your assets. Your beneficiaries will not have to step into the courtroom, if it is set up appropriately. There are no delays. Isn't that what we want for our surviving family members?

Another great benefit of a trust means that your estate and your assets remain private! Legal benefits abound with trusts.

As an example, we hear frequently that wills are challenged in court. Aretha Franklin's and Prince's wills have been challenged. Disgruntled family and friends can come out of the woodwork after death occurs all wanting a share of the assets. Sometimes, those challenges can get ugly. We know that long battles in court eat away at the assets. Trusts are much harder to challenge, and they provide more security for your beneficiaries.

No one wants their family to go through tribulations especially during the grieving period.

> Sometimes it's necessary to have a durable power of attorney in place.

You can have a durable financial power of attorney when financial decisions may be made for you and you can have a durable medical power of attorney. That allows someone to make medical decisions on your behalf when you are unable to do so, as with Alzheimer's.

Another directive that can be used is the Living Will Directive, which helps guide your family members through difficult decisions on your behalf. A directive works in conjunction with the durable powers of attorney. We can help you with all those documents. We include them in our services.

The time to engage a durable power of attorney is when you may be out of the country, or if you're facing surgery, have physical or mental incapacitation. The Living Will working in tandem with the durable power of attorney would ensure that your family members know your desires and would allow them to make the best decisions for you when you can't make them yourself.

Looking at the various trusts you can establish, the revocable trust is something that can be done while both spouses are living. It allows for changes to be made and has the necessary flexibility to meet your needs. Should one spouse die, the trust becomes irrevocable and a separate EIN number must be obtained from the IRS.

A disabled child may be provided for with an irrevocable trust that would establish a set amount for the child without exception.

Normally, a trust can be as flexible as you want or as general, depending on your specific requirements. Life is full of changes and having flexibility helps in estate planning.

Deciding on a trustee to handle the trust is key. The trustee should be someone who will represent the spirit of your trust and manage it in the way you, the owner or the trustor, desires. I don't recommend co-trustees because both trustees must agree on each decision they make. Sometimes that can be problematic. When money is involved, people don't often agree. Therefore, a single trustee is the better option.

A trust can have a little more paperwork involved. If you own a home and it goes into the trust, the trust owns the home. So, you need to file a new deed. Should you sell the home, you must take the deed out of the trust's name and enter the buyer's name. It's not that big of an issue, but it does involve some paperwork.

Being able to put conditions on how your assets are distributed is a major advantage in having trusts. Fees arise when forming trusts, but it's worth it in the long run. By and large, I think the pros outweigh the cons when it comes to trusts.

A definite pro is found in life insurance trusts, which help when it comes to keeping the family wealth secure for succeeding generations.

There must be five hundred different kinds of trusts and I'm sure that you will be able to find the one that best fits your needs. I'd be happy to help.

The biggest mistake people make is not properly funding their trusts. A revocable trust may be established but if there are no assets in the trust, it's useless.

I can't stress enough the importance of estate planning. It's not as complicated as you think. I'd be happy to walk you through it step-by-step. Just knowing that you and your family will be cared for is well worth the effort.

If your estate is planned properly, it will be the greatest I Love You Gift to your loved ones. It's a consummate expression of love and care for those you leave behind.

In the next chapter, we'll wrap things up when it comes to the S.I.M.P.L.E.™ Plan. It's a roadmap to your retirement planning and success!

CHAPTER 10

WORKING TOGETHER TO SECURE YOUR FUTURE

With uncertain times that can have financial side-effects, it's important to work with a financial advisor who has your best interest in mind. Retirement planning may be difficult no matter what.

However, using the S.I.M.P.L.E. ™ Plan as the blueprint to build a solid and secure retirement will alleviate the stress, overcome obstacles and mitigate risk. Having a guaranteed income for the rest of your life will assure you that you can weather financial storms.

I have been a sports and financial coach for twenty-five years. As such, I have developed my people skills so that I may be the best coach possible. It's important to me to know my players and my clients and their goals. I have been blessed with discernment when it comes to guiding people.

You might have guessed that I look at things differently and approach things in a new way. The difference allows me to come at things from a different angle. Financial planning must be done on a person-to-person basis. It's not a one size fits all type of thing.

Your financial success is my goal. Your success is my success! We're in this together. The advice I give my clients has been sound. My track record is excellent, but you don't have to take my word for it. My clients will be glad to give testimony about the advice I've given them.

By continuing my education and staying on top of the latest information and trends, you can be assured that I have the facts you need to make the best decision possible about your financial future. I don't know everything, but I'm willing to find the answers to any problems.

Rest assured that I'm on this journey with you and for you. I don't want my clients to get off the path to success nor to be tangled up by the weeds of incomplete or misinformation. My role as a coach and advocate is something I take very seriously.

I'm there for you. You don't need to live in Louisville, Kentucky, for me to help you. Reach out to me wherever you are. I can help and if I'm not licensed in your state, be assured I will get my license.

Being financially self-sufficient is more important now than ever. With my help, you'll gain confidence and be assured that your future and your legacy are safe for you and your family.

I don't work for any company other than my own. I'm not beholding to any product company. Therefore, I can give you unprejudiced advice about solutions for your financial situation. After we discuss your plans and your goals, we can work together to fill your financial arsenal with the weapons to stave off financial risk and loss.

Together, we can hone your skills, so you'll be able to make the very best decisions about your future. Everyone needs a coach. Everyone needs a mentor who has walked the road before them and who knows the pitfalls and the potholes that are scattered along the way.

We are facing crises in this country that impact our daily existence. Yet, my clients have peace of mind and the confidence that comes with knowing their money is secure despite the various turmoil of life.

Let's find the right strategy for you. Stop by my

website and shoot me an email. I'm there for you! www.learnthesimpleplan.com.

I'd like you to know that you too can have a happy retirement knowing your wealth is protected. So, contact me and let's talk! http://www.apgky.com/.

DISCLOSURES

The information presented in this book represents the personal views and opinions of the author. This information is presented for educational and informational purposes only and is subject to change without notice. The views and opinions of the author have not been independently verified and no representation is made as to the accuracy or completeness of information.

This information is not intended as a solicitation, recommendation, promotion, endorsement or offer of any particular security or other investments. Any and all opinions, commentary, news, research, analyses, website content, or other information contained within is informational only, and does not constitute advice and there are no guarantees associated with them.

The author may represent various firms as an insurance agent, an investment adviser representative, and/or a registered representative. Associated firms, including Registered Investment Advisers, are not liable for any loss, including without limitation the loss of your investment or potential income, which may arise either directly or indirectly as a result of your reliance on the information presented in this book. There is no representation about the suitability of the information presented in this book for your specific investment needs. You should consult your financial professional before acting on any financial strategy or investment product.

The authors of this book are not affiliated with the US government, Social Security Administration, Internal Revenue Service, Securities and Exchange Commission or any other government agency.

INVESTING INVOLVES RISK, INCLUDING THE POSSIBILITY OF THE LOSS OF YOUR PRINCIPAL. Economic factors, market conditions, and investment strategies will affect the performance of any portfolio and there can be no assurance that any specific investment will be suitable or profitable for you.

Comments regarding guaranteed returns or income streams refer only to fixed insurance products and do not refer in any way to securities or investment advisory products or services. Fixed insurance and annuity products and their features, benefits, and/or guarantees are subject to the claims paying ability of the issuing insurance company. You should consult a qualified financial professional regarding all investment decisions.

Made in the USA
Monee, IL
08 November 2026

67994718R00094